Name Your Gates & Take Back Your Cities

Copyright © 2017 by Shiloh Ministries, Inc.

Berlin, Maryland, USA

ISBN 978-0-9890789-3-1

Published by Shiloh Ministries, Inc., in February, 2017

> Scripture quotations marked "NASB" are taken from *The New American Standard Bible®*, Copyright © 1960, 1962, 1963, 1968, 1971, 1972, 1973, 1975, 1977, 1995 by The Lockman Foundation. Used by permission.
>
> Scripture quotations marked "NIV" are taken from the *Holy Bible, New International Version®*. Copyright © 1973, 1978, 1984 by International Bible Society. Used by permission of Zondervan. All rights reserved.
>
> Scripture quotations marked "NKJV" are taken from the *New King James Version*. Copyright © 1982 by Thomas Nelson, Inc. Used by permission. All rights reserved.
>
> Scripture quotations marked "NLT" are taken from the *Holy Bible, New Living Translation*, copyright © 1996. Used by permission of Tyndale House Publishers, Inc., Wheaton, IL 60189 USA. All rights reserved.

All rights reserved. This book is protected by the copyright laws of the United States of America, and may not be copied or reprinted for commercial use or profit. No part of this book may be reproduced or transmitted in any form or by any means – electronic, mechanical or photographic – including photocopying, recording or by any information storage and retrieval system, without prior written permission of the publisher. No patent liability is assumed with respect to the use of the information contained herein. The publisher and authors assume no responsibility for errors or omissions; neither is any liability assumed for damages resulting from use of the information contained herein.

Printed in the United States of America.

Name Your Gates & Take Back Your Cities

This Book Belongs to

_____

Presented by

_____

Introduction

After we prayed all around the Chesapeake Bay, the Lord focused our intercession on the City of Salisbury, Maryland, our regional hub for a 100-mile radius. One of the first things He told us was to pray at Salisbury's gates. Then He asked if we had named them: "The gates of My city had names. The gates of My temple had names. Why don't your gates have names?"

We named the city's four gates according to what they represent. The East Gate is "Truth" because Jesus is the Truth and He will return via Jerusalem's Eastern Gate. The North Gate is "Holiness." Much of Salisbury's commerce occurs there, and the name advocates just measures and true scales in the city's business practices. The West Gate is "Justice" to prevent residents from falling through cracks in the legal system. And the South Gate is "Peace," proclaiming the rule of Christ to adjacent counties in Maryland and Virginia.

We have led intercessors to pray on-site at hundreds of strategic locations around Salisbury, and the results have been remarkable. City officials acknowledge prayer as a leading reason why the crime rate is now its lowest in the 30 years statistics have been compiled.

We began naming gates in other places – city gates, regional gates, national gates. This is equivalent to rededicating the land to God's Kingdom. It is a way of capturing territory from the enemy. Now we are sharing our experiences to encourage readers to do this in their own towns, counties and states. Think what could happen if praying people named the streets/gates where they live!

This is a strategy so simple that even children can do it – learning to think beyond our borders, focus our prayers, and expect tangible results. PRAYER WITHOUT A FOCUS IS LIKE FIRING A GUN WITHOUT AIMING IT.

We encourage you to employ the principles and prayers in this book with anticipation, and look for the outcome!

Blessings of love, peace and joy,
Randy & Barbara Walter

Contents

	Introduction	IV
Section 1	Name Your Gates	VI
Chapter 1	Who Names Your Gates? Why Don't Your Gates Have Names? Significance of Gates Regional Gates	1
Chapter 2	Pray for the Bay "Take Territory" Pray for the Land Ahead of the People Curses on the Land Repentance: Healing the Land White for Harvest	5
Chapter 3	Turning the Battle at the Gates Biblical Examples Seeds of Revival Taking a Region	13
Chapter 4	The Power of Prayer Blessing Rather than Cursing The Spirit of Death The Church isn't Ready "It's God's Time for You"	17
Chapter 5	Possessing the Gates Abraham's Spiritual Heritage The Promise is for Us No More "Business as Usual"	25
Chapter 6	What People are Doing Testimonies from around the Nation and the World	29
Section 2	About Our Father's Business Photos of Prayer at Gates and Prophetic Acts	43
Section 3	Prayer Brochures "Praying Effectively" and "Prayer at the Gates"	54
Section 4	One Seamless Garment Prayers Love the Bride, Harvest, Uncommon Faith, Prayers and Declarations for Places and People	77
	Ordering Books	90

Section 1

Name Your Gates

Chapter 1
Who Names Your Gates?

"If you don't name your gates, someone else will," the Lord declared as we prayed at the head of our street. We had just walked its length – praying and taking Communion at houses whose residents were corrupting the town. At one house, someone was arrested for kiddy porn. Another man on our street would threaten to kill people whenever he was intoxicated. Then one of the largest drug busts in county history occurred on our street when SWAT team members with automatic weapons took down a house and found a huge cache of cocaine.

We had been leading intercession all around the Chesapeake Bay in Maryland, Delaware and Virginia, praying and doing prophetic acts at hundreds of locations. Meantime, in our small town, the street we live on was taken hostage by the enemy, and needed to be liberated. It was several years since we prayer walked our street.

Before leaving our house, we prayed, put on the whole armor of God, took Communion, and pled the Blood of Jesus over ourselves, our property and our family. Standing in our yard, we anointed the soles of our shoes with oil to carry a blessing of peace wherever our feet trod. Then we discreetly took Communion in front of each house of offense, committing a portion of the elements to the ground for the healing of the land. We repented for what had occurred there and what led up to it, and called for the salvation of souls. It was obvious that our prayers were invading the darkness by the language which poured out of the windows of one house.

We walked a half-mile to one end, turned around and walked to the other end, the head/gate of our street where the town war memorial is located. Knowing the importance of praying at gates, we anointed it with the oil of the Holy Spirit, sprinkled salt to symbolize our covenant with God, and took Communion, again committing a

Name Your Gates & Take Back Your Cities

portion of the elements to the ground. Then we asked the Lord to tell us the name of this gate, expecting it to be edifying like the names He had given us for gates in other places.

"The name of this gate is 'Perversion' – until you change it," He said as we listened in shock. "If you don't name your gates, someone else will." We repeated the dedication of the gate and asked the Lord what to rename it. "'Journey,'" He said. "Call everyone on your street onto the journey into the Kingdom of God, or pray them off."

We did as instructed and within the week, people started leaving. The kiddy porn guy and the one who stashed the drugs went to prison. The woman with a large cement gargoyle in front of her house suddenly moved away. A house of hoarders was condemned by the health department, and the residents were forced to leave. We made friends with the guy who threatened to kill people. In all, about seven houses were sold or vacated. We assume that everyone who remains on our street is destined for the Kingdom of God.

'WHY DON'T YOUR GATES HAVE NAMES?'

For years before this, we had been leading prayer journeys about 20 miles away in Salisbury, Maryland, our regional center of influence and commerce. When we started, this small city of 35,000 people was on its way to becoming the nation's fourth most dangerous city for its size. The Lord told us to "oppose a spirit of death in Salisbury," and charged us to name its gates. "The gates of My city had names. The gates of My temple had names. Why don't your gates have names?"

First we had to identify the gates. That was easy. Two major highways intersect in Salisbury. Large signs are posted where each enters the city limits, reading, "Welcome to Salisbury, Crossroads of Delmarva." (Delmarva is a peninsula between

Chapter 1 – Who Names Your Gates?

the Chesapeake Bay and Atlantic Ocean, containing portions of Delaware, Maryland and Virginia.) Our prayer team strategically named Salisbury's gates "Truth," "Holiness," " Justice" and "Peace." To this day, we pray when we enter through one of these gates.

SIGNIFICANCE OF GATES

To take a city for Christ, praying at its gates is vital. In ancient times, the gates were where authorities heard people's causes and rendered judgments. As entrances to marketplaces, gates were often named accordingly ("Sheep Gate," "Fish Gate"). Gates regulated what entered the city. If a gate were breached by an enemy, the city could be captured and its people plundered. Knowing that the enemy comes to steal, kill and destroy, spiritually fortifying city gates is a major defensive strategy. No wonder Nehemiah was so grieved when he learned Jerusalem's gates were "burned with fire."

It is foolish to think we can pray only once or twice. If we let down our guard, the enemy will try to retake the territory we capture from him. So after praying several times at Salisbury's gates, we organized a "Freedom Ride." Two dozen intercessors took a three-hour bus ride around the city limits, declaring blessings, repenting for the city's sin, and singing praises to God. We stopped to pray at each of the gates and the Planned Parenthood office. We spoke light and life to the city, superseding its covenant with death. Our intercession and worship established a wall of righteousness around its borders.

We printed and distributed 200 yard signs which said, "Salisbury, It's God's Time for You. PRAY: Churches come together, righteousness prevail, wells of revival flow."

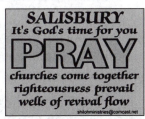

In January, 2017, the mayor of Salisbury announced the city had its "lowest crime rate in history" – lowest number of crimes per capita and lowest number of recorded crimes of any year on record. The chief of police has acknowledged prayer as a major reason. "If it weren't for the

Name Your Gates & Take Back Your Cities

tremendous work you are doing, none of it would be possible," she said.

We have prayed on-site at all the city's public schools and colleges, and at churches, government facilities including police and fire headquarters, the courthouse, crime hot spots, homeless camps, parachurch ministries, and locations known for human trafficking. We prayed for families and fathers, prodigals and backsliders, and declared, "Living water, enter every home," at an artesian well and the municipal pumping station.

We called our campaign "A Time to Love Salisbury."

REGIONAL GATES

Just as cities have gates, so do regions and nations. The Atlantic seaboard is America's Eastern Gate. Its gateposts are the covenants with God affirmed in 1562 by French Huguenots at Jacksonville, Florida, and in 1620 by the Mayflower Pilgrims at Plymouth, Massachusetts. Its doors open and close over the mouth of the Chesapeake Bay.

In 2012, the Lord instructed us to stand on the beach in Ocean City, Maryland, face America's Eastern Gate and proclaim, "No access to terror!" With around 80 intercessors, we declared Psalm 24 over the ocean:

> **Lift up your heads, O you gates!**
> **And be lifted up, you everlasting doors!**
> **And the King of glory shall come in.**
> **Who *is* this King of glory?**
> **The Lord strong and mighty,**
> **The Lord mighty in battle.** (NKJV)

We asked the Lord to enter through the Eastern Gate and release the love, glory and government of God to wash over the land and refresh the people.

Ocean City is the east coast's premier family beach resort. U.S. Rt. 50 begins in Ocean City, horizontally bisects the United States, and ends 3,073 miles later in Sacramento, California. In 2011, intercessors prayed at the eastern end of Rt. 50 and asked the Lord for the name of this gateway to the nation. He answered, *"Destiny."*

Chapter 2
Pray for the Bay

In September, 2007, prior to our Salisbury campaign, the Lord told us to sail across the Chesapeake Bay and proclaim His Word. Then He downloaded a syllabus of Scriptures for us to declare. He said our voices would travel farther over the water than on the land.

On a passenger ferry as we faced each point of the compass, Randy spoke page after page of Scriptures to the land, water and people. We didn't realize until later that we did this on Yom Kippur, the Day of Atonement. A coincidence? We concluded not.

We were to pray for four things prophetically represented by the bay: government, the military, commerce, and the nation's borders.

• **GOVERNMENT**—*The state capitals of Delaware, Maryland and Virginia, plus Washington, D.C., are near the bay.*

• **MILITARY**—*On the bay are the U.S. Naval Academy in Annapolis, the Patuxent River Naval Air Station, the Norfolk Navy Base and numerous other military installations.*

• **COMMERCE**—*The bay has produced a bounty of scale fish and shellfish, including the famous Maryland blue crab. Many communities along its shores have been major exporters of seafood. The bay is also a thoroughfare for commercial ships en route to the strategic seaport and business center of Baltimore.*

• **BORDERS**—*The Chesapeake is the largest estuary in the United States. It empties into the Atlantic Ocean at the nation's Eastern Gate.*

The Lord directed us to "take territory." We were to anoint the soles of our shoes with oil and declare a blessing everywhere our feet trod. Then He said, "Pray for the land ahead of the people, for the

Name Your Gates & Take Back Your Cities

land is more cursed than the people are."

This was totally new to us, so we asked for clarification.

Scripture says the iniquities of the fathers are passed down to the third and fourth generations of their children. Where people are concerned, curses have a prescribed duration. But until the land is redeemed by repentance, it remains cursed as a result of sin, and it hinders men from being saved.

MURDER AND SLAVERY

Europeans settled in the Chesapeake Bay region in 1607, with the founding of Jamestown in Virginia. Over the next 400 years, the land was defiled with many curses.

Most of us are familiar with the account of Pocahontas saving the life of Capt. John Smith. Lesser known is how ruthless the settlers were. Arrogant and brutal, they raided Indian villages, stealing food and killing the very people who had shared their precious stores and kept the English from starving.

This prompted Chief Powhatan, head of the Algonquian-speaking tribes in Virginia, to ask, "Why do you take by force what you can receive through love?" But the pillaging continued, leading to bloody wars between the Europeans and native people.

In 1619, the Virginia governor traded supplies for the first persons of color brought to North America. The 20 Africans who arrived on a Dutch ship had been baptized and given Christian names. They were not slaves but indentured to a limited time of servitude, much as the English colonists who contracted for four to seven years of labor in exchange for passage to the New World.

The unbiblical institution of immutable slavery began in Virginia in 1640, when an indentured African and two indentured Europeans were captured after running away. The Europeans had time added to their indentures, while the African was made a slave for life.

As slavery was mainstreamed, men created in God's image were

Chapter 2 – **Pray for the Bay**

regarded as commodities. Kidnapped from their native lands and robbed of their heritage, slaves could be treated in any fashion their owners thought appropriate. Masters could not be prosecuted for maiming, raping or killing their "property."

The barbarous slave trade mushroomed with the invention of Eli Whitney's cotton "gin" (engine). Demand exponentially increased for laborers to harvest the South's most profitable export.

The abuse and cruelty associated with slavery, which led to the American Civil War, were spawned in the Chesapeake Bay region.

REPENTANCE AND HEALING THE LAND

It was September 22, 2007, when we sailed across the bay. Standing at the rails on the four sides of the passenger ferry to Tangier Island, we declared our Scriptures. Many of them had to do with repentance and healing for the land, in accordance with II Chronicles 7:14 (NKJV), **"If My people who are called by My name, will humble themselves, and pray and seek My face, and turn from their wicked ways, then I will hear from heaven, and will forgive their sin and heal their land."**

The Lord told us to perform a prophetic act by pouring into the bay all of the "revival water" which had been given to Barbara. It came from locations around the world where revivals broke out.

From strategically located Tangier Island, in the middle of the bay, we took a second ferry to the opposite shore. The following day we made the return trip. By then we knew we were to conduct "Pray for the Bay" – not an ecological initiative but a spiritual one, not just for the water and the land but for the repentance of the people on them.

For the first time, we understood the final portion of II Chronicles 7:14, **"...and heal their land."** The land needed healing so people would be free of its curses and could return God to His rightful place in their hearts and in the culture.

When we sailed back across the bay, we stopped again at Tangier

Name Your Gates & Take Back Your Cities

Island. Joshua Thomas, the "Parson of the Islands" of local lore, was born there in 1775. At a time when the outlying islands had no churches and few people could read, the Word of God only came to islanders when a parson visited. Sailing in his log canoe *The Methodist*, Joshua Thomas spread the Gospel throughout the bay region.

At that time, the eastern United States was shifting toward Methodism, which had come out of the Anglican Church. Using newly improvised *methods* to bring people to salvation, "Methodist" ministers declined to wear frock coats or powdered wigs, and broke with tradition by speaking extemporaneously rather than reading their sermons. This freedom was derisively called "enthusiasm" by Anglicans who considered it undignified and disrespectful toward God.

When staid English churchmen would not allow these upstart ministers in their pulpits, Methodists conducted outdoor services that gave rise to the camp meetings which characterized America's Second Great Awakening. Joshua Thomas helped organize the Methodist camp meetings that started on Tangier Island in 1807. Similar meetings had already brought repentance and mass conversions to the Kentucky frontier. Now the same outpouring of God's Spirit was happening on this tiny island so remote that today, its residents still speak with an Elizabethan dialect from colonial times.

As many as 10,000 people from all around the bay would crowd Tangier during the camp meetings. After several decades, the meetings moved to Deal Island, then to Smith Island, where they are still held every July. With the exception of one year when the British occupied Tangier during the War of 1812, the annual meetings have continued. This ongoing connection to the Second Great Awakening is part of the Chesapeake region's spiritual heritage.

DEEP WELLS OF SALVATION

Over the loud speaker, the ferry pilot described modern life on Tangier. The island can only be reached by sea or air. It is so small that people use bicycles, motor scooters or golf carts to traverse its

Chapter 2 – **Pray for the Bay**

10-foot-wide roads. Many residences are cottages with small fenced yards, very close together. For generations, its main industry has been commercial fishing.

To obtain municipal water in the middle of the salty bay, the island used six 1,000-foot-deep artesian wells. That's deep! An artesian well needn't be pumped, only tapped, because its water is under pressure. We saw this as symbolic of the deep wells of salvation which once flowed on Tangier, and we prayed those spiritual springs reopen to again bring living water to the region.

MODERN-DAY REVIVAL

A reprise of the camp meeting spirit occurred on Tangier in 1995. Swain Memorial United Methodist Church and the independent New Testament Church overcame their differences of 50 years and shared their resources for a series of meetings. During a six-week revival, 217 of Tangier's then 700 residents returned to the Lord or made first-time professions of faith. Among them was James "Ooker" Eskridge, who became a spiritual leader and mayor of the island.

During our layover on the return ferry trip, we met with Ooker and asked about vestiges of the revival 12 years later. He said little evidence of that spiritual harvest remained. Crab shanties around the harbor, which once abounded with signs about faith in Jesus, no longer bore that witness – except for one, Ooker's. Many of the converts returned to their former ways of life. Another outpouring of God's Spirit was needed.

We told Ooker our plan. During the first four months of 2008, we would mobilize our Shiloh Ministries e-mail network of more than 300 people to pray for the bay region. Then in May, we would organize a journey to Tangier for intercessors to pray with the islanders.

Starting in January, 2008, we sent out e-mails every two weeks, containing prayer points and prophetic messages. They also included historical insights for spiritual mapping – identifying places where sin opened the door for the enemy to steal, kill and destroy. This

Name Your Gates & Take Back Your Cities

provided direction for prayer and repentance to cleanse locations of curses and restore the land. The Lord told us to pray specifically that churches come together, righteousness reign, and the wells of salvation flow freely.

We made a pilgrimage to Joshua Thomas' grave on Deal Island to pray that God again release the spirit of repentance which made his ministry so fruitful. Leaning against his cement burial vault was an oyster shell, probably dropped by a seagull to access its contents. It was the only one we saw in the cemetery. We took it with us.

JOSHUA RUN

After nine e-mails, it was May 3, the day we led the "Joshua Run." Forty-three intercessors, some from as far away as Florida and Pennsylvania, boarded the ferry to Tangier. Nineteen people who came from a distance stayed in our home that weekend.

We all took Communion on the 75-minute cruise. Extravagant praise and worship was conducted as we sailed. It was highly significant that this occurred *on the water*.

When we arrived at the dock, the islanders said they heard us coming. We walked to the Methodist Church to pray with residents. One of the islanders was overheard to say, "I've *never* been to a prayer service like that." Afterward we had sweet fellowship over a meal. Then it was time to depart.

Randy had the oyster shell from Joshua Thomas' grave. On the return trip, in an unscripted prophetic act, we anointed it with oil and passed it around so everyone could pray over it. When the shell came back to Randy, the Spirit prompted him to throw it into the bay and declare, "Revival to the shellfish!"

CRABS AND OYSTERS

Ecologists, government agencies and the media had all sounded the death knells of the Chesapeake Bay for many years. Due to pollution, they said, watermen would need to find another way to

Chapter 2 – **Pray for the Bay**

make a living because the crabs and oysters were dying out.

Eleven days after the Joshua Run, Ooker called to say, "Crabs are runnin'." That was significant because May, 2008, was cold and damp. Ooker fishes for softshell crabs ("peelers"), which usually don't "run" until the weather is hot and sunny.

He said crab pots that normally produced 15 or 20 peelers contained 50. Ooker and other watermen could see the bay floor was "crawling with crabs." Crab runs, which normally went for a week, lasted for three. All this took place in Tangier Sound, the portion of the bay where we worshiped God and threw in the oyster shell.

LARGEST HARVEST IN LIVING MEMORY

Tangier watermen caught so many crabs that their shanties weren't large enough to hold them, so they took some to neighboring islands. Commercial canneries in nearby Crisfield received so many crabs that they reportedly bought up the region's supply of kiddie pools to keep them in. Not only the quantity but the size of the crabs increased. It was the greatest crab harvest in living memory.

After crabbing season ended, watermen refitted their boats to go out for oysters, which were also making a conspicuous comeback in Tangier Sound. Many of the fishermen sat out previous winters because of the dismal oyster catch. But that year, Ooker would later tell us, "Every man caught his limit."

Unlike crabbing season, when the abundant harvest went largely unreported in the media, the return of the oysters was publicized. Government officials and environmentalists took credit, saying it resulted from conservation and stricter regulations. But the islanders and those of us who prayed for the bay know it was really God who did it.

That September, a pastor who grew up in Crisfield asked if we heard what happened there Labor Day weekend. Of several dozen churches in the area, all but a couple came together for a special holiday service. Organizers optimistically hoped 500 people would turn

Name Your Gates & Take Back Your Cities

out; 700 came. They were prepared to conduct a few baptisms and ended up doing around 50. The pastor, who received our Pray for the Bay e-mails, said he thought this was because of the prayers that churches come together, righteousness reign, and the wells of salvation flow freely.

WHITE FOR HARVEST

In each succeeding year, the crab catch in the Chesapeake has continued to increase in volume, and has spread to other parts of the bay. Oysters have followed suit. As we reflected on this, we knew it was symbolic of something yet to come. When we asked the Lord about it, He said—

"What I did was not to provide a livelihood for the watermen on Tangier, as much as I performed a prophetic act of salvation to the bay. What was the word I had you use when you threw the oyster shell into the water? 'Revival.' You spoke revival, and your authority was validated because the crabs are having a revival. The oysters came from the other church to join the services. If you can speak it to the shellfish, you can speak it to the people."

The 17 million people who then lived around the Chesapeake Bay were the focus of this project. As we spoke revival over them, Jesus' words in John 4:35 (NKJV) came to mind—

"Do you not say, 'There are still four months and then comes the harvest'? Behold, I say to you, lift up your eyes and look at the fields, for they are already white for harvest!"

Chapter 3
Turning the Battle at the Gates

We are all called to the ministry of praying at our gates. Don't we want to crush the head of the enemy and repel him from our cities and towns? It is better to wage the battle at the gates, rather than try to remove him after he gets inside our walls. This is as important for our families, neighbors and city as when we intercede for them individually. No one is excluded from this assignment.

Let's look at some of the people in the Bible whom God used to turn the battle at the gates. We know none of their names.

In II Kings 7 (NKJV), God used four leprous men – the most despised and ostracized of people – to save a city. They were sitting at the gate of Samaria, which was under siege by Syria and suffered such a great famine that some of its inhabitants resorted to cannibalism. These lepers reasoned that they would die if they remained in the city, and decided to surrender to the Syrian army. **"If they keep us alive, we shall live; and if they kill us, we shall only die,"** they said.

So at twilight they went to the enemy camp, only to find no one there. **"For the L**ORD** had caused the army of the Syrians to hear the noise of chariots and the noise of horses – the noise of a great army; so they said to one another, 'Look, the king of Israel has hired against us the kings of the Hittites and the kings of the Egyptians to attack us!' Therefore they arose and fled at twilight, and left the camp intact – their tents, their horses, and their donkeys – and they fled for their lives."**

Finding the place deserted, the lepers ate and drank and started looting the camp. Then they realized it was wicked not to share with the starving city, and journeyed back to bring the news. Fearing a trap, the king sent a small party to check the lepers' story. They saw

Name Your Gates & Take Back Your Cities

discarded weapons and garments abandoned by the Syrian army in its haste, and found the camp just as the lepers described. So the people of Samaria plundered the camp and the city was saved.

The battle turned when God used four lepers at Samaria's gate to rescue the entire population. Isaiah wrote, **"The Lord of hosts will be... for strength to those who turn back the battle at the gate"** (Isaiah 28:5-6 NKJV).

WOMEN SAVED CITIES

II Samuel 20 tells of Sheba's rebellion against King David, who assembled an army to pursue him. As they prepared to attack the city where Sheba holed up, a wise woman there asked them why they would **"swallow up the inheritance of the Lord."** If the city delivered Sheba, David's army would relent. The woman told the people, and they killed Sheba and threw his head over the wall. Then the army withdrew and the city was saved.

Another woman, in Judges 9, saved her city of Thebez by dropping a millstone from its strong tower onto the head of King Abimelech, crushing his skull as he fought against the city. Towers were customarily located over or next to the gates.

The names of these women are not reported but their legacy is, because they turned the battle at the gates.

TRANSFORMATION

Just like the women and the lepers, God will use any of us who are willing. Think: If each person in a small church would pray at the head of their streets/gates, what might God do to eradicate sin and pave the way for souls to be saved, backsliders to return, families to be healed, and drug addicts to be delivered?

What if they renamed other streets in their town or city? And then declared the name of that gate every time they traveled on that street? Maybe they are streets where children live, or the supermarket or police department is located. Or in underserved parts of town.

Chapter 3 – **Turning the Battle at the Gates**

Think of the transformation that would take place!

Barbara dreamed she was in Salisbury at an Episcopal Church, and she and the priest took the Sunday school children out to name three gates in the small area around the church. In her dream, the children came up with the names for the gates. Barbara and the priest just chaperoned. Children need to name gates too. It is so easy.

Everyone doesn't have to give these gates the same names. Gates can have many names. The greater the number of righteous names, the better. This is capturing territory and advancing the Kingdom of God.

Where we live on the Eastern Shore of Maryland, there are many little towns and small churches. In a 60-minute drive, we can put our feet on the ground in five towns. If each of these towns had 20-50 intercessors naming their gates, what a regional shift would occur! Let's do it!!!

SEEDS FOR REVIVAL

Barbara had a passion for intercession years before she knew what to call it. In 1983, she began to pray from 9 a.m. to noon, four days a week, at The Son'Spot, Ocean City's Christian coffeehouse. She posted an invitation for people to join her, and occasionally some would. But most of the time she was by herself. She renamed that street Glory Street, fully expecting to see new street signs.

The Son'Spot was able to buy the building it met in, and another of the five properties on that street also became a Christian outreach. Thousands of people from around the world have been saved on Glory Street. Could it be that those prayers, declarations and renaming the gate were seeds for revival?

Every Friday for at least one year, Barbara asked others to join her and pray at the region's only full-time Christian radio station. Even though not many responded, fervent prayers were offered up for several hours each week.

Name Your Gates & Take Back Your Cities

Then Barbara asked people to accompany her as she prayed in different places all over Delmarva. Every Thursday she went to the town the Lord showed her. Many times on that evening's news, we would see the answer to things that were prayed about.

Randy was working and unable to join them. His job was to cover them in prayer as they prayed. One week, Barbara and another intercessor went to a town where high school students were making suicide pacts. In a short period of time, many children took their lives. The prayer warriors interceded on the premises and the suicides stopped. Other people no doubt were praying, but it is important to pray on-site.

Now it is Barbara's habit to pray for over 600 people every morning. Many of them are our grandchildren's friends. When they visit with our grandkids and we feed them, they are delighted to hear they're being prayed for.

TAKING A REGION

After the Lord told us to sail across the Chesapeake Bay and pray on the water in 2007, the two of us traveled thousands of miles to pray in hundreds of strategic places all around the bay. Many times, others prayed with us. We prayed often in Washington, D.C., sometimes preparing the way for major events and ministries there.

Not everyone can traverse a region to pray, but everyone can find time to pray on their street and in their town. As often as possible, it's important to pray on-site with feet on the ground, taking territory and bringing a blessing.

In the book of Nehemiah, each family took responsibility to repair and rebuild the wall and gates nearest their houses. Nehemiah 4:6 (NKJV) says, **"The people had a mind to work."** We all have the responsibility of protecting our cities.

Chapter 4
The Power of Prayer

We had driven all around the Chesapeake Bay, interceding at hundreds of locations for the land and the people, and hammering Scripture-covered surveyor's stakes into the ground we claimed for God's Kingdom. So it was surprising when He instructed us to make our next prayer focus the city of Salisbury, only 20 minutes from our home.

When we asked the Lord to clarify our assignment, He reminded us of Salisbury's importance as the Lower Eastern Shore's center of influence and supply. It is the "Crossroads of Delmarva." From a spiritual warfare perspective, it is a highly strategic location.

In January, 2010, we led our first tactical prayer blitz through Salisbury. A blizzard, rare for this area, struck on the day of the prayer journey. We proceeded with our plans, depending on God to keep us safe in the snow. After briefing the 10 hardy participants, ages 12 to 81, we dispersed to Salisbury's four gates.

BLESSING RATHER THAN CURSING

Operating beyond the practice of binding and loosing, we taught our prayer teams how to declare the blessings of Scripture over the city. God said in Isaiah 55:11 (NKJV), **"So shall My word be that goes forth from My mouth; it shall not return to Me void, but it shall accomplish what I please, and it shall prosper in the thing for which I sent it."**

We spoke light and life to Salisbury in place of darkness and death. We repented for the sins of the residents and their ancestors, took Communion and sowed some of the elements into the ground for the healing of the land. We prayed that God cause His grace to abound to Salisbury and pour out His Spirit over the city.

Name Your Gates & Take Back Your Cities

"BACKSLIDERS RETURN" and assorted Scriptures were written on rocks and left at strategic places during one of our Salisbury prayer incursions, in which we prayed for fathers and families.

Salisbury's gates are at the city limits of its east-west and north-south highways. Large signs stand in the median strips, saying, "Welcome to Salisbury, Crossroads of Delmarva." By the time our four teams reached the gates, it was 22 degrees and the blowing snow was rapidly accumulating.

These signs are somewhat inaccessible, especially in a snowstorm. We figured the intercessors would park nearby and pray in their cars. But no, they prayed at the signs. On busy U.S. Rt. 50, the group which included one of the eldest intercessors walked across the snow blanketed highway, danced at the sign in the median,

Chapter 4 – The Power of Prayer

celebrated the Lord's Supper, and made their declarations over the city. They came back so excited because they felt the power in what they did. The other groups shared similar accounts when we reassembled to debrief.

The two of us had prayed at the southernmost gate. After pronouncing blessings over Salisbury, we took Communion and declared Jesus' death, Resurrection and Second Coming. We committed a portion of the bread to the ground, then poured out some of the juice. Drifting snow quickly covered the purple stain, and Randy heard the Lord say concerning Salisbury, "Though your sins are like scarlet, they shall be as white as snow" (Isaiah 1:18 NKJV).

When we shared our experience with the group, everyone came to the same conclusion: The snow represented the extent to which the city's sin will be cleansed. God was preparing Salisbury for its redemption.

ANOTHER SIGN

In December, 1931, Matthew Williams was lynched on the courthouse lawn in Salisbury. An enraged mob snatched him from the hospital, where he was being guarded after killing his white employer earlier that day in a dispute over wages. Williams' corpse was dragged through the black section of the city as a warning, then it was set afire. The incident made national headlines. Despite the convening of a grand jury, no one was ever indicted for the crime.

When Williams was murdered at the place where justice was to be dispensed, a curse was released. Even if others had already repented on this site, we believed we should go in the authority God had given us for our Salisbury assignment, and add our prayers to those prayed before. We went in April, 2010, after praying with students during Christian Life Week at Salisbury University.

On the old courthouse steps, we confessed this crime on behalf of the city, and pleaded for mercy for the sins of racism, hatred, and the murder of Matthew Williams. We took Communion and prayed that the land be healed. We took authority over undercurrents of

Name Your Gates & Take Back Your Cities

prejudice which still exist today on the Eastern Shore, especially in light of the Hispanic and Asian subcultures here. We prayed for reconciliation among all races, including Native Americans.

While we prayed, sunlight passed through the globe of a lamppost and created the perfect shape of a dove on the sidewalk, much as when light is concentrated through the lens of a magnifying glass. We took it as a sign that God was responding to our prayers.

As we asked forgiveness for the Jim Crow spirit of segregation that opposes unity, crows landed in the surrounding trees and cawed. Then we prayed for righteousness to reign in the city and county governments; an outpouring of God's Spirit over the courthouse and elected officials; and that the judgments of God shape rulings and policies of the courts and city/county councils.

We took authority over a spirit of poverty, and prayed for the region to come into spiritual prosperity. By this time, the crows were so numerous and noisy that we could not hear the traffic on busy U.S. Rt. 50, a half-block away.

Folklore attributes prophetic significance to crows, as though their calls were spiritual proclamations. That's where the expression "to crow" comes from. We believe those crows were relaying our declarations for all Creation to hear.

THE SPIRIT OF DEATH

By the time of our next prayer journey in October, Salisbury had experienced seven murders that year. It was a high number for such a small city. Had our opposition to the spirit of death there been ineffective? That's what the enemy would have us think, so we asked God.

The Lord answered by quizzing us, "What happened when demon-possessed people were brought to Jesus?" Randy answered that they convulsed, foamed at the mouth and shrieked.

"Do you know why?" the Lord continued. "The demons

Chapter 4 – **The Power of Prayer**

manifested because they knew they had to leave." He told us not to be discouraged but to keep pressing in with authority to evict the spirit of death from Salisbury. It was manifesting, He said, because it knew it had to leave.

Several dozen of us gathered at a church on a Saturday, took Communion and prayed for our safety. Then we deployed in groups for intercession at strategic locations throughout the city – police and fire headquarters, the courthouse, municipal offices, the hospital, the first free African American church in Salisbury (located at the junction of its major highways), the Planned Parenthood office, the river, and key points bordering the city's high crime area.

We prayed that the covenant of life purchased with the Blood of Jesus supersede any covenant the city had with death. We invited Jesus to bring God's love, government and glory into Salisbury. We prayed for city officials and employees, emergency responders and businesses, churches and pastors.

"FIRE"

Three intercessors joined the two of us at our location. Next to us was a huge church which takes up an entire block. On the sidewalk, we took Communion and released the love of God in place of a root of bitterness. Randy looked down and on the sidewalk was a laurel root which none of us noticed previously. Laurel is one of the toughest roots to dig up. We took it as a sign that God Himself was uprooting bitterness from that economically depressed part of the city.

While we were praying, a girl approached and asked if we had seen a jean jacket. Her fair complexion and red hair were very out of place in this neighborhood. We told her that the Lord knew where it was, and asked Him to help her find it. As she continued retracing her steps and disappeared around the corner, we asked the Lord to be her covering. She returned very excited, her coat under her arm. She was the only person we encountered during the entire time we prayed there.

Name Your Gates & Take Back Your Cities

Randy asked how we could pray for her, and she shyly told us about herself. She was 20 years old, a drug addict and prostitute. Her child was being raised by someone else. As she confided in us, we kept loving her. Barbara proclaimed she would be fire for God. Surprised, she said "Fire" was her street name.

The Lord told Randy to seal her as His own. With her permission, he traced a cross on her forehead with anointing oil. Then God spoke of His love for her and His desire to give her a future without the pain of abuse and addiction. Tearfully, she produced a rosary from her purse and placed it around her neck.

THE CHURCH ISN'T READY

We took her to a fast food restaurant, and she requested a Bible. After dropping her off, we went to a nearby church in search of a Bible. No one was there. We went to a Christian business but it was closed. We found another big church with someone inside. Randy told the man we needed a small Bible for our new friend. After looking through a storage area, he produced an old Bible with a hole worn in the cover. It was the only one he could find in that big church.

Fire was still waiting when we returned. Barbara gave her the Bible and a kiss, and told her she could call us anytime. We never heard from her again.

When we rejoined the other groups for debriefing, we shared our impression of this prophetic experience: Many of us are praying for revival, but the Church isn't ready for the harvest.

We had asked Fire if she wanted to go back to our church base with us. She didn't, but what if she did? What if we had encountered four or five people and took them back? Our meeting was scheduled to end at one o'clock. What would we do with them afterward?

If prostitutes and drug addicts came to our churches one Sunday and needed help, what would we do? We all need to get ready if we want revival.

Chapter 4 – **The Power of Prayer**

"IT'S GOD'S TIME FOR YOU"

In 2011 after Randy retired, praying for Salisbury became our top priority. Being from a neighboring county, we needed to acquaint ourselves with the inner workings of our regional metropolis. We attended a Safe Streets meeting where we met the mayor and chief of police and told them about our assignment. They encouraged us, and the chief of police asked us to consider enrolling in the Citizens' Police Academy, an eight-week course which familiarizes participants with department operations.

When we filled out the application, we listed as our reason for taking the course, "to know how to better pray for the city and the police department." The course showed us how to stand in the gap for the city police, county sheriff and deputies, and state troopers. We gained a new appreciation for how sacrificially law enforcement officers work to protect and serve our communities.

After we met members of the city council during a "Stop Hatin'" march at Salisbury University, we began attending council meetings as silent intercessors and peacemakers. It was important not to draw attention to ourselves as we prayed.

Randy called 55 churches in and around the city to see which ones held weekly prayer meetings where it would be appropriate for the public to pray for Salisbury. Fourteen did. Another 14 said they did not. Six could not be reached and the remainder did not respond. We attempted to attend two prayer meetings that were advertised and no one was there. At one church, we prayed by ourselves anyway.

We started taking pastors to breakfast. We asked what they thought God's vision is for Salisbury, and what they believed an outpouring of His Spirit over the city would look like. One pastor candidly acknowledged that he was too busy doing visitations and overseeing church activities, plant maintenance and other administrative tasks. He hadn't thought about the bigger picture. He announced his intention to begin having his congregation pray for

Name Your Gates & Take Back Your Cities

other city pastors and churches each Sunday during worship.

FREEDOM RIDE

On June 25, 2011, we followed the Lord's next instruction and facilitated a Freedom Ride around Salisbury to pray at its gates.

When God told us what to name the event, Randy researched Freedom Riders during the Civil Rights Movement. Black and white passengers rode interstate buses into the segregated South, challenging Jim Crow laws which, among other things, institutionalized racism by prohibiting people of different colors from sitting together on buses. Blacks were required to sit in the back. The Freedom Rides were conceived to set captives free and proclaim liberty to the oppressed.

It turned out that the day we received this directive was the 50th anniversary of the first Freedom Ride. It was a reflection of biblical Jubilee, meaning "The Year of Liberty," when debts were forgiven, slaves and servants freed, and the land was given rest to restore its fertility and improve future harvests.

ONGOING ASSIGNMENT

The book is still open on Salisbury. Our goal is not just to focus on symptoms such as crime, but to remove the causes. The Lord told us not to view praying for Salisbury as a one-time initiative but an ongoing campaign. He said—

"Prayer takes faith because it takes time. If prayer got instant results, everybody would do it whether they believed it or not. Everybody looks for a quick way to get what they want. If the world could use Me as a vending machine, don't you think they would pray? So there is more to prayer than just getting what you want. It enables relationship. Prayer has a function beyond needs because it produces intimacy."

To mobilize an army of intercessors, we wrote two brochures, "Praying Effectively" and "Prayer at the Gates," which appear later in this book.

Chapter 5
Possessing the Gates

Used with permission of Sid Roth's "It's Supernatural!" Original article at http://sidroth.org/articles/possessing-gates/, March 23, 2006. Author unknown.

The book of Genesis records two instances where the descendants of Abraham were given this spiritual heritage: "Possess the gates of your enemies."

The first instance is in Genesis 22:17 (NASB), right after the LORD has provided a substitute sacrifice for the life of Isaac. An angel of the LORD calls out blessings to Abraham from the LORD because Abraham did not withhold his son from the altar.

Among the blessings, he declares, **"And your seed shall possess the gate of their enemies."** In other words the seed, or the descendants, of Abraham shall possess the gate of their enemies.

Then a few chapters later this same promise is made to the descendants of Abraham's son Isaac through his wife Rebecca. In chapter 24, verse 60, the relatives of Rebecca send her away with the servant of Abraham, to become Isaac's wife. As she is leaving, they speak this blessing over her:

"May you, our sister, become thousands of ten thousands, and may your descendants possess the gate of those who hate them" (NASB).

Rebecca becomes the carrier of this promise, which is so similar to the one God spoke over Abraham and Isaac in chapter 22. Since Rebecca is about to marry Isaac at the end of chapter 24, we could say that the two promises regarding "possessing the gate of your enemy" are about to "marry" and be passed on to their offspring.

What power! What a multiplication! What a confirmation, as

Name Your Gates & Take Back Your Cities

the same thing is spoken by the mouth of two witnesses!

Isaac and Rebecca have twin sons, and one of them, Jacob, is the ancestor of the Jewish people. So we can certainly say that this powerful promise of possessing the gates of the enemy is something available to Jewish people even today, if they walk in it by faith.

But what about the rest of us, who are not physical descendants of Jacob? Glad you asked that question.

Let's look at Galatians. 3:29: **"And if you are Christ's, then you are Abraham's seed, and heirs according to the promise"** (NKJV).

The previous verse says that there is neither "Jew nor Greek" – neither Jew nor Gentile – in Messiah Yeshua. We are all one in Him, without distinction.

And if we belong to Him, we are Abraham's seed. So we inherit all the promises spoken to Abraham's seed in the Word of God, including the promise to possess the gates of our enemies.

Okay, but what does that promise mean for us today? To answer that question, we have to consider how gates functioned in Bible times.

Most of the cities or large towns of those days were surrounded by walls of some kind – anything from a kind of stick fence to thick and high stone walls with parapets for defense. The idea was to be able to protect the inhabitants at night from animals which might wander in and most of all, to protect the city from marauding humans – thieves, bandits and conquering armies.

The gate or gates to these enclosures were the only way into or out of the city. So all commercial traffic entered and exited through the gates.

Thus the city gate became a place for all kinds of important activity in the life of the city and its inhabitants. The area near the gate became a literal marketplace, where commodities from farmers outside the city were bought and sold. (II Kings 7:1; Nehemiah 12:25).

Increased commerce gave rise to disputes. So the gate area

Chapter 5 – **Possessing the Gates**

became a place of adjudication – municipal law courts (Isaiah 29:21; Amos 5:15; Zechariah 8:16). The city elders (respected men, not simply "old" men) would sit in the gate area and bring the wisdom of their experience and insight to settle commercial disputes and other matters affecting the life of the city's inhabitants.

The elders and those passing through the gate area would also discuss the issues of the day and the issues of life, sometimes setting policy for the city and advising the city's ruler. This in turn gave rise to the gate area becoming the center for political activity and even for mustering militias (Judges 5:11).

Kings would sometimes sit in the city gates, both to dispense justice and to take the political pulse of the people (II Samuel 19:8). Here's a good example of that from I Kings 22:10:

"Now the king of Israel and Jehoshaphat king of Judah were sitting each on his throne, arrayed in their robes, at the threshing floor at the entrance of the gate of Samaria; and all the prophets were prophesying before them" (NASB).

With kings and commerce and courts congregating at the city gate, no wonder the gate also became a place for public declaration by prophets and others. In the case of Jeremiah's prophetic ministry, the LORD several times told him to stand in the city gate and proclaim the word of the LORD (Jeremiah 7:2; 17:19). We could say that the city gate was the media center for ancient cities, as well as their commercial center.

The gates to a city, then, represented a point of power, a place to exercise control over that city. A military conqueror would try to get control of the gate in order to enter the city most easily. A king who had the hearts of the elders who sat in the gate would politically control the city. A person who organized and ran the commercial market and storehouses at the gate would control the economic life of the city – and its surrounding villages.

At the gate, ideas and policies flowed along with the commerce.

Name Your Gates & Take Back Your Cities

These ideas could result in the rising or falling of rulers and even nations.

And that brings us to the modern day in which we live. In our lives – in our cities, states, nations – it often seems like an enemy of the Kingdom of God has possessed our "gates." This enemy represents ideals and principals contrary to those of Heaven's Kingdom. Yet they influence our business life, our cultural life, our social life, our political life – even our church life.

And what God is saying to us today, I believe, is, "Rise up and possess the gates of your enemies. Stop settling for the status quo. Take My promise and take back your culture."

I believe He is saying to us – yes, even to us intercessors – to go out into the marketplace. Go out to the places of power, where the decisions of government are made. Go out into the business community. Go out into the judicial system and the legislature, the political arena. Take these places for the Kingdom of God.

Are you sensing that maybe the Lord is repositioning you right now? Are you sensing that He has a new assignment for you outside the prayer closet where you've labored these many years?

If so, then you are not alone. I believe He has been teaching many of us how to live in and by His Spirit, so that He could send us out in such a time as this into the "gates" and change what goes on there.

No more "business as usual." A new day is dawning. And it is the Army of the Lord that is taking territory, that is moving the boundary stones in this earth until they agree with the decrees of Heaven.

This is what it means to be salt and light. Yes, prayer is necessary. Yes, strategic intercession is powerful and valuable. Yes, contemplative intimacy is the cry of the Lord's heart for us.

But for some of us it's time now to take what we learned in the place of hiddenness and go into all the world.

Go then, and every place where the sole of your foot treads, take territory for your King!

Chapter 6
What People are Doing

For many years, we have regularly prayed for our town of Berlin, Maryland, plus Salisbury to our west and Ocean City to our east. Berlin (population 4,000) was named "America's Coolest Small Town" a couple years ago. A friend from out of state said he believes it was due to our years of interceding and prayer walking our streets.

In 2016, prayer helped reduce crime in Salisbury to its lowest rate since the city started keeping records. And in 2015, the resort town of Ocean City (summer weekend population can top 300,000) was the safest it has been in 25 years. Serious crime dropped by 45 percent, the lowest since the '90s.

Think of what could be done in your town, your area. In a small church of 20-50 people, suppose everyone would name the street they live on? What if they prayed for and renamed two additional streets? That could be up to 150 streets/gates claimed for Jesus.

Imagine how your town could be changed by prayer. Schools, churches, government, businesses and infrastructure all need prayer.

Has anyone prayed for the gates of your state capital?

TESTIMONIES

We are excited to relate some of the responses to our August 20, 2016 Elijah List post, "Name Your Gates and Take Back Your City." Replies came from people in 25 states plus Africa, India, the Middle East, Australia, Nepal and South America.

Many of these people have far exceeded what we have done, and we are learning from their strategies. What brilliant ideas God has given them! After reading these accounts, think what you can do, either as one person or as a group.

Your Gates & Take Back Your Cities

LOUISIANA

Friend Kenny Cox is a retired Army officer who was awarded The Soldier Medal for heroism at the Pentagon on 9/11. He now serves in the Louisiana legislature. His wife, Candie, coordinated pastors and leaders in their parish to go out in teams and name their gates. They first did this in their small town, then took it to a nearby city of 250,000 people. Pastors, mayors, police chiefs, sheriffs and legislators enthusiastically participated.

KENNY & CANDIE COX

They strategically mapped out their prayer targets, took Communion as a group, and anointed the soles of their shoes before they left. Then they divided into 8 teams to pray at the 8 gates they identified. The chief of police wanted to go first and name his gate. He called it "Prosperity." A drug-infested area was named "Redemption."

When they returned, documents listing every participant and the gates they named were sealed in a glass container and placed in the town safe by the mayor. Pastors are instructing their congregations to pray blessings for their city whenever they enter through one of its gates. As people learn this new practice, Kenny said, "repetition creates perfection."

NORTHERN CALIFORNIA

"In the last four years, our quiet neighborhood here in Northern California had taken a turn where it was not so quiet any longer. A once-friendly neighborhood where there were waves of neighborly kindness had become a neighborhood of resentment and separation.

"After learning of your ministry, I began praying over the gates to my neighborhood and things began to change. The malicious, vindictive individuals were eradicated from my immediate area.

Chapter 6 – **What People are Doing**

"As I walked my dog, I would pray against certain activities I knew were going on at a particular residence, and began speaking names of 'Truth' and 'Life' upon them. People fled from these residences!

"A satanist is now separated from the source of the chaos and mayhem that was in their house and life. A drug-addicted mother who was wreaking havoc upon her two young children and ailing husband was now out of the picture and getting the help she needs.

"A household that harbored the spirits of false witness is now at peace. At another home, adult promiscuity is no longer a normal lifestyle because of God's mighty hand and the assurance of prayers being heard!

"God bless you and your ministry! This is so powerful, and every church should have this ministry to combat the enemy in every zip code." Francine Huerta

GIRDLETREE, MARYLAND

Belle Redden, 84, from the tiny rural town of Girdletree, Maryland, named the road going toward the town of Stockton the "Trusting Gate" because, she said, "we need to trust our neighbors. It used to be, years ago, there was always a rivalry between Girdletree and Stockton."

She named another road the "Love Gate" so there would be love between neighbors. As newcomers move onto this street, she is watching them form special relationships as her prayer is answered.

MUSKEGON, MICHIGAN

Pastor Tim Cross in Muskegon, Michigan, said he will apply this principle in his area, where 30-plus churches each take one day a month to pray 24 hours for their county. When he initially presented the idea of 24/7 intercession to pastors at a luncheon, the prosecutor, police chief and mayor all "begged" for prayer. After three years, crime has dropped by 20 percent. County leaders credit prayer for the decrease.

Name Your Gates & Take Back Your Cities

"I take crimes in my county personally," Pastor Cross said. He asked the police chief and mayor, "How can we help you?" They were so grateful. He led the mayor to the Lord, and now the mayor vacuums his church every week. Pastor Cross gave the prosecutor his first Bible and started having Bible studies with him.

"The priests should be anointing the kings," said Pastor Cross. Now the city holds prayer meetings with its politicians. "Jesus wept over Jerusalem and has a heart for cities," the pastor said. "The battle now is to keep the momentum going."

STEVENSVILLE, MARYLAND

When we prayed at the Chesapeake Bay Bridge on January 10, 2016, we were joined by Neill and Mary Ann Russell, along with Pastor John and June Pringle and members of their family, and people from their church. On the way home, the Russells saw an unusually brilliant double rainbow. People later told us it was also seen in Ocean City, 100 miles away.

We prayed at the Bay Bridge because it is a gate which regulates what comes onto our peninsula. Neill, a public school teacher in Annapolis, crosses the bay bridge almost every weekday to go to work. Ever since we prayed, he and others have noticed police pulling over motorists on both sides of the bridge like never before. Most of these stops are obviously for drug trafficking. He attributes that to our prayer in January.

PENNSYLVANIA

Ruth walked the grounds of her church compound and prayed against prejudice as she approached a gate named "Mercy." That entrance was formerly called "Prejudice" because on fair days, it was the site of a booth which sold Confederate flags. The Lord showed her she was watering the ground as she walked, and she must do it regularly so the water can soak in and reach the roots. "So I became a conduit to the outpouring of the Holy Spirit," she said.

Chapter 6 – **What People are Doing**

As she continued walking, she reached a rubbish dump. "God opened my eyes to some beautiful flowers growing there which I hadn't ever seen before. He told me these are the outsiders, the people that society has discarded, the people coming to the food closet, the people with huge needs. I feel like He told me to collect some of the seeds and plant them in the rectory garden and care for them!

"I noticed poison ivy strangling the trees, and God spoke to me about gossip and how poisonous it is, and to stay far away from it. I got on my knees and repented for my own part and also on behalf of the church for these sins."

Love Your Cities

FLORIDA

In her book *Preparing for Battle*, Kim Johnson tells how hurts were dictating her attitude toward her city. Even though she is an internationally recognized intercessor and worship leader, the Lord called her a hypocrite "because you rally people to pray for your city, even for your mayor, but you despise where you are. You are mad at the city. You have despised the land. It should be the powers and principalities that are ruling over it that you should be dealing with."

Kim wrote, "We cannot go to war for something we don't believe in… We are called to take dominion where God has planted us on this side of eternity."

NEW YORK CITY

Chris Myers' Trinity Church in New York City was challenged to "be the Church," and go out to pray for the Upper East Side. Twelve groups of 6-12 people prayed at specific locations and for firefighters, police, students and business owners in those neighborhoods.

"This summer, the Ground Takers (99 Trinity folks) prayed and

Name Your Gates & Take Back Your Cities

fasted throughout the city for six weeks and covered over 2,000 blocks across 48 neighborhoods and all of the boroughs but Staten Island. This was the culmination of blanketing the city with prayer. We continue to pray over our city and invite the Holy Spirit to revive our city spiritually."

WEST OCEAN CITY, MARYLAND

Sara named her street "Love" and saw an immediate change in her husband. She also named every single room in her house, even her garage, with the nine fruits of the Spirit. What a great idea!

ANCHORAGE, ALASKA

Teri Lundy, from Anchorage, Alaska, is praying over her city. "We did this many years ago in Sitka, Alaska. We renamed the old and new gates there. It was a training season and we saw God's heart move in response to prayer, basically doing what you described in your article. I believe the Lord put your article for me to read today to confirm His assignment.

"I took two women with me to the gates of Anchorage and taught them how to reclaim the gates of the city: Repentance at the first gate only. We used salt, made decrees, 'planted' Scripture on Popsicle sticks into the ground, and anointed everything. We renamed several gates.

"They had never done anything like this and were a little embarrassed at first by my loud decrees and shofar declarations. But now they want to join me as we venture and prepare for part two: going to all the neighborhood gates.

"I've been in Anchorage eight years. It has been a culture shock. I am isolated, but my Father sent me here to this north place far away from my whales, otters, salmon, sea lions and beautiful sea. It has been rough. In the last 1-1/2 years or so, the violence and shootings have escalated to the point that people are vocalizing fear and calling Anchorage 'Los Anchorage.' There was even a town meeting

Chapter 6 – **What People are Doing**

where individuals from all over the city gathered, wanting something done. The scale of death and fear is very new to this place.

"When the Lord told me to pray over the city, I didn't know where to begin! A small town, sure, but a city? In January, 2016, the demon tried to kill me. Now I know why. In the middle of the night came two words, 'The Gates.' FINALLY! A plan from my Father!! So I kept praying and two women wanted to go.

"We used Psalm 24 at the first gate, renamed 'Dena'ina Gate,' honoring those native people who gathered in the area of the first gate to hunt and fish, and to celebrate and thank the Creator for His provision.

"There is a lot of work to be done here by three women! It would be awesome to train teams to go on assignment in their local communities. Right now I'm gathering up gang names and areas they 'rule' on my map. This is huge here. Jesus wins."

TANGIER ISLAND, VIRGINIA

Spencer and Mildred Johnson moved to the tiny, remote island of Tangier, Virginia. Located in the middle of the Chesapeake Bay with a population of under 500, this is where Mildred grew up. She remembers the residents as friendly when she was young, so the Johnsons named the main street "Hospitality and Kindness."

TANGIER ISLAND'S 10-ft.-wide Main St. is now named "Hospitality" and "Kindness." Less than 500 people now reside on Tangier.

Name Your Gates & Take Back Your Cities

Spencer and Mildred didn't just *name* the gate, they are *doing* it. They started putting out on a table, free for the taking, clothing and other items left behind by previous residents of the house they bought. They open their home and feed hungry children, to whom they are teaching the Gospel. They embody the song lyrics, "Don't speak of love, show me."

LEBANON, THE MIDDLE EAST

"I have prayed so heavily for the strongholds to be brought down over my city and my nation, I even prayed fervently for America (I live in Lebanon). 'Father in Jesus' name I call upon the hosts of heaven to go over this spot – 800 miles around and 800 miles across – and shred, pull down, destroy and burn all strongholds, principalities and the powers of darkness ruling from the second heaven, take down their platforms, lock them in a box and send them into a dry place to be tormented day and night. In Jesus' name, I receive it.'

"As a result of my prayers, things started to manifest in Lebanon. As I prayed to rip the veil off darkness and all deceptions, lies and corruptions of the enemy, the army started to uncover terrorist cells where radical Islam and what derives from it like ISIS and Al-Nusra took refuge. They launched many waves of attacks against them, taking them down. Security increased, especially in my area. Many corrupt plots and deceptions were starting to uncover as drug lords started to get exposed. I don't claim that I was the only one changing things. I do know things were starting to happen at the same period of time when I started to push forward my warfare.

"I prayed so many times over America and its allies. I prayed for Persia, for its people to be saved; and of course against all strongholds and principalities like the one that stopped the prayers of Daniel in ancient times. I also practiced the One Seamless Garment Prayer*, and whenever I traveled from the city to the mountain where my original home lies in the country, I would command the hosts of Heaven to pull down all the strongholds and platforms of darkness and torch the demonic influences and actors over mosques.

Chapter 6 – **What People are Doing**

I got hold of the One Seamless Garment prayer that I used many times to pray over America, Lebanon and Persia, so that Cyrus would be revealed again through the new President, Mr. Donald Trump.

"I prayed over the gateways of my spirit. I also prayed and called on the hosts to shut down the gateways of hell on the four borders of the historic Promised Land, which today encompass many nations. I prayed over the gateways of America to shut them down, and renamed them 'Love,' 'Salvation,' 'Majesty' and 'Greatness.'" Rabih Antoine Slim

* The One Seamless Garment prayers can be found in section four of this book.

SEATTLE, WASHINGTON

A Seattle bridge popularly called "The Aurora Bridge" is also known as "Suicide Bridge," where 230 suicides occurred plus many other lives lost due to accidents. Kristina Biro renamed it "Hope."

"My son, his friend and I were visiting one of the tourist attractions under the bridge, 'The Troll.' Busloads of tourists

NOTICE THAT "THE TROLL" has a car in its left hand.

come to see this.... The Lord asked me to anoint the ground where this statue is and one of the pillars that holds up this bridge. I asked the Lord what the current spiritual name of the bridge is. Two words came from the Lord: 'delusion,' a false idea or belief that is caused by mental illness; and 'derision,' the use of ridicule or scorn to show contempt."

Name Your Gates & Take Back Your Cities

"After declaring this land and bridge belongs to Jesus and pleading His Blood, I asked the Lord what the new name of this bridge is. One word came again. 'HOPE'! I joyfully went home praising God for what He is doing there. The highway running over this bridge also has a new name, praise God! 'HOPE HIGHWAY'! It runs past Seattle's downtown waterfront to our airport, through some of the most crime-ridden hot spots of our city."

Kristina drew a map of the city's gates, major highways, bridges, schools, hospitals, fire and police headquarters, to pray at each location. She listed businesses in her neighborhood to visit each owner "as the Lord leads, praying and pouring oil in their restrooms. We have two public parks here, one high school, one elementary school, four churches. I am joining our neighborhood's community council....

"Our neighborhood's current spiritual name is 'Division.' No wonder it's so hard to get our block watch group together! I anointed and prayed at one boundary of our neighborhood, and went to each corner of that intersection. Prostitution, crime, drugs, adult dancing and escort services are on this street.... My anointing oil vial on my key ring is full and ready! Woo hoo! Go God!"

AUSTRALIA

Mary Rose, 84, from Australia, said, "The Lord is continually talking of establishing His Kingdom here on Earth, and you people are doing very important preparation."

HOUSTON, TEXAS

Neysa Briggs and her Advance Team of intercessors have prayer walked Houston, the surrounding areas and the whole state of Texas for many years. They pray seven days for each gate. "We identify God's gates by the defilement – cleanse them with the Blood, ask God to seal them from the demonic, and we invite the angelic in....

"We have 30 ladies and one gentleman on our team. We don't all go at one time – that's just an impossibility. Plus, you can't be as

Chapter 6 – What People are Doing

mobile and 'unobvious' as you sometimes need to be. So we try to make sure that each person going is the exact one with the right giftings that God wants on the land at that time.

"There has been lots of victory for the Kingdom. We really believe this could impact Houston – spiritually and even commercially."

RENO, NEVADA

Debra Munoz, from Reno, e-mailed, "How would I take back the gates of my health?"

What a great question. We never thought about this. God is expanding our concept of gates from nations, cities, streets, homes and rooms, down to our personal beings. After praying about this, we realized that many health issues come about through poor eating habits, negative speaking, lack of discipline in our thinking, and not guarding our eye and ear gates from negativity. So we named our mouth gates "Self-control" to regulate what goes in and what comes out. Our eye gates are "Purity" and our ear gates "Good Reports." Our other senses/gates of touch, smell and taste we call "Righteousness, Peace and Joy." You can name your personal gates anything you want.

NEPAL

"My mother got the revelation about our land that blood was shed in anger and the same spirit of anger is causing conflict, verbal accusation, blaming, pornography, disagreement between spouse and family member, recurring feelings of divorce and separation, insecurity, addiction. Our marriage needs restoration. We don't do anything together except abuse each other verbally. I always feel it's a spiritual attack and have been seeking help. It's really a challenge for me as I run prayer house, and work as a leadership trainer for pastors and leaders."

OUR RESPONSE: Many Christian leaders are being attacked because of curses on the land. When curses are removed by repentance (II Chronicles 7:14), people are free to restore God to His rightful place in their hearts and in the culture.

Name Your Gates & Take Back Your Cities

BALTIMORE, MARYLAND

"We prayer walk on a portion of a corridor where our church is located. We partner with the police major of our district to identify areas where there are heavy activities of crime. Thank God there haven't been any major crimes since we began our prayer walks. Also, we prayer walk in front of city hall in Baltimore twice a week. I love the strategy of putting oil under our feet and partaking in Communion." Sabrina Sutton

VIRGINIA

While visiting Tenerife, Canary Islands, the Lord led Raylyn Terrell and her son up a volcanic mountain. "There, at the direction of our Lord, we took Communion, making proclamations, declarations and decrees as I turned north, south, east and west. Territory proclaimed included the whole Mediterranean region, all of North Africa, Western Russia, the Middle East, Atlantic Islands, and the Eastern United States. Finally I buried in the shallow soil under a bush, tooth picks to which Scripture passages were attached on small bits of paper. I claimed every scriptural promise that the Lord showed me, wrapped all in a plastic baggie and buried the holy package."

NEW MEXICO

Amy Ruleen in New Mexico anointed the gates of her subdivision called Tierra del Sol (Land of the Sun), renaming it "Land of the Son." Many houses in her neighborhood have been for sale but none sold. Owners got frustrated and took down the signs.

"I spoke to two vacant ones and commanded them to be sold. The first one had a spirit called 'Death of Dreams' on it. The man who started it in the '80s never finished it. He finished the garage and lived in it until his death. The main house is still unfinished and now is not up to code. I spoke to it, bound that spirit and commanded a new family that had money and resources to repurpose it – redefine, redesign and love it.

"To the second house, I spoke a fun, faith-filled family that

Chapter 6 – **What People are Doing**

would create energy and life. Praise Report: Three days later, I drove by it and there was a SOLD sign on it. Hallelujah!"

Amy identified underlying problems in her town of Alamogordo (White Sands). "Our town is on the verge of death. We all know it and it is talked about often, and now there is fighting between the people and the government as our town draws its last breaths. I know my assignment is to stand in the gap for marriages, family and this town. Thank you for any insights you may have."

OUR RESPONSE: Your town has no vision? Without a vision the people perish. In our prayers for Salisbury, we pray that the pastors receive and act on God's vision for the city. Begin to verbally bless your town. Sometimes we ride through towns and declare blessings for every business, neighborhood, government building, church and school. It might not be too late but it will take work. Speak light and life to your town. God loves your town and its people and the land.

VIRGINIA

Bill Fisher, in Virginia, prayer walked and renamed all the streets/gates in his rural 50-home Stonehenge development, now called "Chief Cornerstone." Stonehenge Way is now "Christ's Way." He made stakes to drive in near the present signs with new spiritual names on them: "Awakening, River of God, Restoration."

Bill e-mailed, "Men, women, boys and girls see an old man with a walking stick, 'MY TOKEN ROD OF AUTHORITY,' that he doesn't use, only carries. I walk by every day, except for rain. I pick up all trash and try not to be seen doing it.… Jesus lives in this 78-year-old and loves this community and people.

"There are lots of divine appointments along the way. I'm gradually meeting people. I call the streets by their spiritual names and see their destinies fulfilled before it happens. An open heaven is the goal. What an honor, responsibility and commission."

Wow, people are reclaiming the land city by city, street by street, even room by room. Keep on going, troops! You are God's

Name Your Gates & Take Back Your Cities

intercessors. Take back territory from the enemy and advance the Kingdom of God.

LEWES, DELAWARE

Eileen and Scott Campbell prayed over the gates/intersections in their development, called Heron Bay, for the Lord's "blessing and intervention in any evil." Eileen wrote, "After these prayers, I have noticed some changes – no multiple groups living in one house, less carousing up and down in golf carts, and even less card parties in the clubhouse. I am going to say it was God's action."

BALTIMORE, MARYLAND

Tina Young was led by the Lord in dreams and visions to pray at the Turkey Point Lighthouse. She e-mailed, "Generations of people before who had prayed and interceded and sought the Lord on our behalf had been silenced.... I saw in the Spirit, the old wells being opened and the prayers of these saints rushing out as though the people themselves were rushing past me over the water.

"When we were on the point praying, I heard to rename this place 'Safe Harbor.' I had never really heard of renaming a place before and I knew this was the Lord. When we were going to the parking lot, we saw a sign that said this place was to be a harbor of safety."

Her group also renamed the Ft. McHenry Memorial "Freedom"; named two spots overlooking a highway "Freedom" and "Blessing"; an elementary school "Purity"; and a college "Virtue."

TRAVELING THE NATION

Retired physician Frank Pisciotta, from Baltimore, traveled to the four corners of our nation plus Canada to pray, make declarations and drive in Scripture stakes, lifting curses and claiming the land for Jesus Christ.

He left in 2012 on the Jewish holiday Rosh Hashanah, and returned from his two-week prayer blitz on Succoth, driving 1,000 miles a day.

Section 2

Photos

About Our Father's Business

> ### *The Lord said to us:*
> "You are replenishing the earth with your faith, your declarations and your steadfastness. That affects both the ground and the people on it. Don't forget that you've marked your territory with your surveyor's stakes, claiming the land for Me."

Name Your Gates & Take Back Your Cities

We conducted our second Freedom Ride in 2015.

IN LOUISIANA, pastors, public officials, police officers and intercessors, led by Kenny and Candie Cox, enthusiastically prayed at and named the gates of their city.

About Our Father's Business

On our first Freedom Ride in 2011, intercessors put their feet on the ground at Salisbury's four gates and Planned Parenthood office to speak life to the city and break covenants with death.

PRAYING AT SALISBURY MIDDLE SCHOOL – Five pastors joined our second Freedom Ride, praying at every public school in Salisbury.

Name Your Gates & Take Back Your Cities

SALISBURY MAYOR JAKE DAY receives the spiritual key to the city from Randy as representatives from city churches pray.

PRAYING IN ANNAPOLIS, Maryland's capital, with Revelation 22.

About Our Father's Business

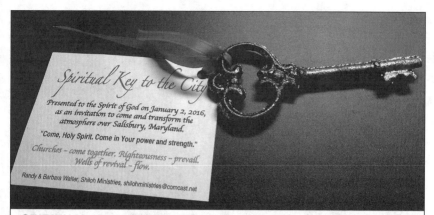

SPIRITUAL KEY TO THE CITY was presented to the Spirit of God on January 2, 2016, as an invitation to come and transform the atmosphere over Salisbury, Maryland. "Come, Holy Spirit, Come in Your power and strength." Church – come together. Righteousness – prevail. Wells of revival – flow.

WE JOINED Jon and Jolene Hamill of Lamplighter Ministries, and Robert and Annette Stagmer of Revelation 22 Alliance, at the Rt. 50 bridge in Ocean City to pray for this "Destiny" gate to the nation.

Name Your Gates & Take Back Your Cities

INTERCESSORS from around the bay met in Ocean City for a solemn assembly in 2012 to pray at America's Eastern Gate.

PRAYING AT THE CHESAPEAKE BAY BRIDGE with Pastor John and June Pringle and members of New Life Christian Outreach.

About Our Father's Business

WE PRAYED and made declarations over America's Eastern Gate at the mouth of the Chesapeake Bay, at the Bay Bridge Tunnel.

PREPARING TO PRAY OVER HUMAN TRAFFICKING in Baltimore with members of Woodlawn Christian Fellowship, in Gwynn Oak, pastored by Tom and Michelle Perrera.

Name Your Gates & Take Back Your Cities

MEETING AT THE MALL to strategize before going out to pray.

WORSHIP AND PRAYER for fathers and families, in Salisbury park.

About Our Father's Business

COMMUNITY PRAYER time before Salisbury Area National Day of Prayer Breakfast included clergy, business leaders and students.

PRAYING AT 8 downtown churches representing every denomination in Salisbury.

ALAS, WARMER WEATHER as we joined Robert and Annette Stagmer of Revelation 22 Alliance when they prayed for Maryland at every county courthouse in the state.

Name Your Gates & Take Back Your Cities

GATHERING BEFORE WE PRAY AT SCHOOLS IN OUR COUNTY

EACH YEAR we pray at all public schools in our area before they open.

About Our Father's Business

PRAYING AT STRATEGIC PLACES IN SALISBURY

ON A COLD DAY, we prayed at the facility that supplies Salisbury's municipal water – for living water to enter every home in the city.

Section 3

Prayer Brochures

IF My people who are called by My name will **humble** themselves, and **pray** and **seek** My face, and **turn** from their wicked ways…

God's Answers

Praying Effectively

Seeing the Bigger Picture…

Mobilizing a Prayer Army

Our Prayers

THEN I will **hear** from heaven, and will **forgive** their sin and **heal** their land.
(II Chronicles 7:14 NKJV)

TOPICS

- *Pray? Why?*
- *Why mobilize a prayer army?*
- *What is a gap? What gives a legal right?*
- *Types of intercessors – where do you fit?*
- *Strategic prayer*
- *How do we pray effectively?*
- *What are prophetic acts?*
- *Prophetic acts in the Bible*
- *Unified prayer heals the land, brings revival*
- *When God's Law is transgressed...*
- *Where and when to pray*
- *Prepare yourself*
- *The Blood of Jesus*
- *Tools for prophetic acts*
- *What to pray*

Pray? Why?
BECAUSE IT WORKS!

Of course you pray. Almost everyone does. But look farther, wider, higher; see the bigger picture for the restoration of the land and the people. This is prayer of vision.

The intent of Jabez' prayer (I Chronicles 4:10) was that God bless him, enlarge his territory *and cause him to be a blessing to others.* God granted his request.

Will God use our prayers to bring revival? Every great outpouring of the Holy Spirit has begun with prayer.

Each one of our prayers is like a drop in a bucket. Every drop counts. Our prayers are being added to all the righteous prayers which have gone before us, to fill the bowls in Heaven.

"…[T]hey were holding golden **bowls full of incense, which are the prayers of the saints**" (Revelation 5:8 NKJV).

When these bowls are filled to overflowing, they reach a tipping point at which God pours out His Spirit on a people and their land.

Why mobilize a prayer army?

- To heal the land
- To prepare the way of the Lord
- To humble our hearts in repentance
- To entreat the Lord to send revival

"If My people who are called by My name will humble themselves, and pray and seek My face, and turn from their wicked ways, then I will hear from heaven, and will forgive their sin and heal their land" (II Chronicles 7:14 NKJV).

Will you sit on the fence or stand in the GAP? Christians *are* held accountable for what happens in their sphere of influence (neighborhood, church, town, nation and world).

"'So I sought for a man among them who would make a wall, and stand in the gap before Me on behalf of the land, that I should not destroy it; but I found no one'" (Ezekiel 22:30 NKJV).

Shedding of innocent blood, broken covenants, immorality, idolatry, witchcraft

People who are lovers of themselves, lovers of money, boastful, proud, abusive, disobedient to their parents, ungrateful, unholy, without love, unforgiving, slanderous, without self-control, brutal, not lovers of the good, treacherous, rash, conceited, lovers of pleasure rather than lovers of God (II Timothy 3:2-4 NIV)

STANDING IN THE GAP, HOLDING BACK EVIL

What is a gap? What gives a legal right?

A **gap** is someplace that lawlessness has gained a foothold, such as where drugs, prostitution or violence are prevalent. By man's disobedience – particularly shedding of innocent blood, immorality, witchcraft, idolatry and broken covenants – evil spirits are given a **legal right** (permission to enter from the land's occupants) to create a **gap** in God's protective covering. Even seemingly small things like jealousy, slander, gossip, hatred, fear, division and lies give a **legal right** to the enemy.

Then Satan can send confusion, sickness, financial problems and other calamities to cause people to suffer loss.

Evil spirits can only go as far as they have a **legal right**. Targeted prayer and holiness create a boundary line which they cannot cross.

THE LAND IS CURSED BECAUSE OF...

Innocent blood: *Abortion, murder, fatal accidents, war*
Immorality: *Promiscuity, adultery, perversion, pornography*
Witchcraft: *Manipulation, occult rituals, drug abuse*
Idolatry: *Putting things or people ahead of God*
Broken covenants: *Divorce, lying, violated agreements*

"The earth is defiled by its people; they have disobeyed the laws, violated the statutes and broken the everlasting covenant. Therefore a curse consumes the earth; its people must bear their guilt" (Isaiah 24:5-6 NIV).

God puts a canopy of protection and blessing over an area when His children humble themselves by praying, and live consistent, holy lives.

Satan is powerless over any situation where God's people have forgiveness and love for one another. Forgiving is Christlike.

IT WORKS...
The Lord made a place of safety for the Hebrew children in the land of Goshen.
(Exodus 8:22-23)

Types of intercessors – where do you fit?

There are different types of intercessors, just as an army has different kinds of troops.

Warrior intercessors do exploits. They forcefully take territory from the enemy. They are like...
Spies – undercover agents who report enemy strengths and weaknesses so an effective attack strategy can be developed.
Shock troops – seasoned fighters who know how to capture territory; they lead the attack and establish a beachhead.

DRIVE-BY SHOOTERS

In Baltimore, a team of three "mothers of the church," each over 65 and more than 300 pounds, chose to do a drive-by shooting instead of a prayer walk. They inquired at a police station where the precinct's most violent crime areas were, informing police they intended to pray at these hot spots and fully expected to see a change.

At each location, they proclaimed the Word of God, prayed for change, squirted anointing oil out of mustard bottles onto the ground, and declared Jesus Christ is Lord. They never got out of their vehicle.

Returning to the police station six months later, they were told that crime at these hot spots dropped 50% since they prayed. An excited major asked them to pray at additional locations. Beware of old ladies with mustard bottles.

Maintenance intercessors may pray by themselves, yet their intercession is essential for success. They are like...
Mop up troops – reinforcements which secure and defend captured territory against a counterattack.
Occupation forces – they establish government and enforce the new ruler's laws.

Jesus said to occupy until He returns. That is the job of the churches, ministries and praying families.

What kind of intercessor do you think you are?

Strategic prayer

Every Christian needs to be involved in strategic prayer. Little is accomplished without a strategy.

WARFARE STRATEGIES

✸ *Know your enemy:* "[W]e are not fighting against flesh-and-blood enemies, but against evil rulers and authorities of the unseen world…" (Ephesians 6:12 NLT).

✸ *Spiritual mapping:* History (i.e. occult practices, broken treaties, murders) and current activities (such as drug dealing, adult establishments) reveal the origin of curses. These are places to pray for repentance and cleansing of the land.

✸ *Have nothing evil in you:* Satan had no foothold or authority in Jesus' life. Jesus said, "The ruler of this world… has nothing in Me" (John 14:30 NKJV). Check your heart for things like unforgiveness, resentment, bitterness, self-pity, jealousy, accusation, anger, rebellion, pride.

✸ *Wear your body armor:* Belt of truth; breastplate of righteousness; being sure-footed with the Gospel of peace; shield of faith; helmet of salvation; sword of the Spirit, which is the Word of God (Ephesians 6:13-17).

✸ *Weapons:* Prayer, God's Word, love and prophetic acts.

Pray for the Bay

In 2008, 43 people sailed to the strategic location of Tangier Island *(spiritual mapping)* to pray with residents following four months of intercession for the Chesapeake Bay region. After a day of praise and prayer for repentance and revival, an oyster shell was anointed and thrown into the bay *(prophetic act)* as the intercessors shouted in unison, "Revival to the shellfish!"

Eleven days later, Tangier's mayor reported the bay was "crawling with crabs." Despite gloomy government predictions, it was the best crabbing season in living memory. Afterward, oystering followed suit. The harvest of shellfish is believed to be a foreshadowing of a harvest of souls.

How do we pray effectively?

• Effective prayer is characterized by earnestness and fervency. This kind of prayer is miracle-producing, informed, deliberate.
• We can't pray effectively when we are ignorant of the truth.
• One person can turn the tide so God will cleanse the land.
• All prayer is good. Effective prayer is better. Corporate, effective prayer is best.

"But I don't pray well…"

• God uses unlikely vessels. Compared to Jesus, we all pray like children. He said the only way to enter God's Kingdom is like a little child. God can use your heart regardless of your skills.
• God is honored, not bothered, when we ask Him about our smaller (as well as larger) concerns.
• We won't receive answers unless we pray. If every person did his job, the whole world would be won to Christ by now.
• It's okay if you don't feel spiritual – you might be more effective. Sometimes when you feel spiritual, you act religious.

9 *drunk men* – Barbara's Story

Nine very loud, vulgar, angry, drunk men were seated near us in a restaurant. I complained in my heart, resentful that they were ruining our dinner. As I prayed that someone would make them leave, I remembered the Lord told me that morning not to complain or I would lose my blessings.

Adjusting my attitude as we finished our meal, I realized the Lord loved those men. I asked Him to bless them. Then a love welled up in *my* heart and I asked the Lord to help *me* bless them. I told my husband I was going over to their table, and his prayers covered me.

"Gentlemen," I said, "Jesus loves you and I'm going to pray for you. Let us take hands." After I pointed at the only man who resisted, we all took hands and I said a brief prayer for them, their families and their work. I ended with a cheerful "God bless you." The men became peaceful and the whole atmosphere changed. Love was the strategic weapon.

What are prophetic acts?

You probably do prophetic acts every day. They are faith gestures intended to produce godly outcomes. They can be discreet rather than showy or brash, done anywhere, anytime.

A prophetic act calls things which are not as though they were (Romans 4:17). You can transform an everyday function into a prophetic act by adding a physical expression to a prayer mind-set. There is greater faith as you go from being an intercessor with a request to an agent who helps bring it to pass.

Attempting a prophetic act in a non-serious or disrespectful way can bring an unpleasant outcome. Prophetic acts are spiritual warfare – aggression against the enemy. If you don't do them seriously and righteously, you're open to attack.

TRY DOING THIS...

√ Taking a meal to a sick neighbor is an act of kindness. Praying that it brings encouragement and does more than satisfy physical hunger transforms it into a prophetic act.

√ When you pray in your home for the nation and its government, it's intercession. When you do the same thing on the U.S. Capitol steps, it's a prophetic act.

√ If you bring stones back from Israel, you could put them on a shelf, look at them and feel blessed by them. But if you plant them in strategic places, it becomes a prophetic act.

√ Pronounce a blessing over your house that extends to everyone who sets foot on your property of crosses your threshold.

√ Pray at and place oil on the entrance to your workplace.

√ Anoint your tires, praying everywhere you drive will be blessed.

IT'S A PROPHETIC ACT IF YOU PRAY...

√ For the President as you watch him on TV.

√ For children's protection when you see a school bus.

√ For peace and lawfulness every time you pass a police station. *If you take Communion on the station grounds and bless the building, it's a more powerful prophetic act.*

√ As you walk, believing everyplace your foot treads is being captured unto obedience and ushered into the Kingdom of God.

Prophetic acts in the Bible

- Baptism and Communion are powerful prophetic acts. Baptism is symbolic of repentance; Communion is symbolic of forgiveness.
- Naaman had to wash himself in the Jordan River seven times to be cured of leprosy (II Kings 5).
- Moses cast down his staff before Pharaoh and it became a serpent.
- Lamb's blood was put on the Hebrews' doorposts for the death angel to pass over them.
- The ultimate prophetic act was Jesus' Crucifixion.

> Prayer = power.
> Prayer + prophetic act = more power.
> Prayer + prophetic act + unity among believers = most power.

Unified prayer heals the land, brings revival

EXAMPLE: *Unity of Vision*

A great revival occurred in Hemet, a California town where bikers, gang members and drug manufacturing were prevalent. When pastors and churches began praying together, crime became almost nonexistent as the churches filled with one-time outlaws. A righteous, prosperous, happy community was born out of territory which once belonged to Satan.

EXAMPLE: *Repentance Healed the Land*

Crime in a Guatemalan town was so bad that it had four jails. Drunkenness, violence and abuse were rampant. Families were falling apart. The churches came together for unified, strategic prayer and people repented of paganism. Soon, all the jails were closed. People swelled the churches. They began to prosper after putting aside a poor work ethic which kept them in poverty. God healed their land. Their harvests became bountiful, with carrots the size of a man's forearm, and they bought Mercedes trucks to transport their produce.

When God's Law is transgressed...

• The ground ceases to yield its strength (Genesis 4:12).
• The land "vomits out" its inhabitants (Leviticus 18:25) through famines, wars, tornadoes, hurricanes, floods, wildfires, earthquakes, volcanic eruptions, instability of governments, poverty, divorce (fatherless children, families destroyed), plagues, cruel oppression, etc.

Where and when to pray

• This is a call to the corporate Body of Christ to pray at homes, churches and schools. Pray when you see school buses, prisons, municipal buildings, bodies of water, bridges, highways, entrances to cities, etc. *This is spiritual homeland security.*

Prepare yourself

• Pray as a team when possible.
• Pray the Blood of Jesus cover you, your family and team.
• Pray your hearts be broken for the lost.
• Have peace. It is God who does the work; you are just His tool.

The Blood of Jesus

• "Without the shedding of blood there is no forgiveness" (Hebrews 9:22 NASB). A blood sacrifice atones for the sins which bring curses on the land. Jesus paid the sacrifice with His own Blood, once and for all. It must be accepted and invoked.
• The power and authority demons have over geographical areas is broken by repentance and celebrating Communion anywhere you pray. Jesus said, "Do this in remembrance of Me."
• Scatter some bread and pour out some juice on the ground to rebuke Satan with the New Covenant sealed with Jesus' Blood.
• Redeeming the land works by the finger of God and by Jesus' redemptive work on the cross. It is dangerous even to suggest that redemption is obtained by any other power.

Tools for prophetic acts

• Take Communion elements, anointing oil, blessed water, salt.
• It is God who redeems the land; He uses us as tools. Rituals alone don't do it. Perform whatever prophetic act you have faith for. Ask the Holy Spirit to show you what to do.

What to pray

• Pray at strategic sites for righteousness to prevail, churches to come together, and wells of salvation to spring forth.
• Pray for repentance, healing, revival and protection in your region and across the nation.
• Declare that Jesus Christ is Sovereign Lord over the territory.
• Confess your sins and seek forgiveness for the nation's sin.
• For the Body of Christ and for pastors, pray encouragement and bind discouragement, discontentment and despondency.
• Pray for ministers to love souls and proclaim God's Word.
• Pray for angels to be gatekeepers and fight against evil spirits.
• Pray that revelation of disobedience and rebellion bring forth repentance and lasting fruit of righteousness that pleases God.
• Command what is in darkness to come into the light.
• Declare to the Church: "Wake up! Come alive!"
• Declare to the backsliders: "Return to the Lord!"
• Remember that prayer and repentance accomplish the same thing as water poured on parched land: They bring healing. Once the land is healed, men's hearts will be released from the curses of the land. Then they are free to return to God and give Him His rightful place in their lives.
• Revival is not just when unsaved people come into the Kingdom of God; it is when people in the churches forsake their secret (and sometimes not so secret) sins. To that end, repentance is as important as seeing souls won to Christ.
• Ask God to rain down with extravagance His grace, mercy and love.

Prayer at the Gates
Taking Back Your City and Region

AWAKENING • REVIVAL • TRANSFORMATION

Lift up your heads, O you gates! And be lifted up, you everlasting doors! And the King of Glory shall come in. *Psalm 24:7 NKJV*

Be **ALERT, FLEXIBLE, AVAILABLE**

TOPICS

- *Message from the Lord*
- *Implementation*
- *Be Spiritually Clean: Repentance*
- *On-site Strategy: Prayer at City Gates*
- *On-site Strategy: Declarations for a City/Region*
- *On-site Strategy: Neighborhood Prayer Walks*
- *On-site Strategy: Hospitals and Medical Facilities*
- *On-site Strategy: Schools and Universities*
- *Prayers for Reconciliation of the Races*

Message from the Lord about Intercession

"The most important thing about prayer is confidence. That doesn't mean to be full of yourselves. Your confidence isn't in yourself anyway. You have authority to ask and declare, and God will open the portals of Heaven to hear and respond.

"What needs prayer? Where are the strategic places to capture enemy territory? How many troops will you need, and how will you get them?

"The problem with most prayer meetings is, even when people go to pray for needs beyond their household, very few have a sense of expectation. It becomes like any other church meeting – a requirement for appearing holy.

"I whittled down Gideon's army because there is a difference between soldiers and warriors. A soldier is somebody who puts on a uniform. A warrior seeks out the battle and anticipates victory. Among Gideon's men I weeded out the timid and the followers – those who were obeying out of a sense of duty but had no heart for the fight. What remained? A tiny core of committed men who were not amateurs that got in the way.

"How does someone go from soldier to warrior? (1) Desiring to see the Kingdom of God advance. (2) Praying to have a hunger for holiness and a desire to serve God, to loathe evil and desire good. (3) Having a vision for territory. (4) Recognizing that authority comes from God's Word and not men's performance. (5) Knowing with assurance that the Word of God puts the enemy to flight."

Implementation

> "You will also declare a thing, and it will be established..." (Job 22:28 NKJV).

• Reject fears of personal inadequacy – success depends on the power of God's Word, not on us.

• Conduct intercession with humility and discretion, not out of a sense of self-importance.

• War is fought over territory. Determine what territory the enemy possesses and take it back.

• Pray on-site. It is very powerful to place your feet on the land and intercede at locations where it is needed.

• What needs prayer? Look for evidence of enemy occupation: drugs, violence, poverty, corruption, disrespect for authority, theft, ineffective ministries, social strife, etc.

• Determine strategic places to declare God's Word: city gates, state lines, schools, courthouses, police and fire headquarters, TV and radio stations, airports, military installations, historical locations, churches, bridges, crime hot spots, places where traffic accidents occur frequently, etc.

• Ask, "What would You have us do, Lord?"

• Try to enlist other intercessors.

• As often as possible, pray on-site with at least one other person.

• Confess any sins, faults or unforgiveness you are aware of, that your prayers not be hindered.

> "Who may ascend the hill of the Lord? And who may stand in His holy place? He who has clean hands and a pure heart..." (Psalm 24:3-4 NASB).

- Plead the Blood of Jesus over yourselves, your families, your property and your vehicles. Make sure the enemy has no authority or legal right to retaliate against you.

- Whenever possible, go on prayer journeys with others to guard one another and benefit from each other's insight and wisdom.

- Believe you have the authority to declare God's Word and promises in prayer. Be God-confident, not self-conscious.

- As a child in the household of God, believe that He has heard and is answering your prayers, even if you don't see immediate results.

- As Daniel identified with the sins of his nation, we have authority and responsibility to repent for things done by others.

- Our prayers are being added to others being prayed, and to the prayers of generations before us, that the bowls of intercession in heaven might be full to the tipping point.

> **"Violence will not be heard again in your land, nor devastation or destruction within your borders; but you will call your walls salvation, and your gates praise."**
> Isaiah 60:18 NASB

Be Spiritually Clean Before You Pray

REPENTANCE

Father, forgive us for—

- not honoring others in the Body of Christ, and for not recognizing their work for the Kingdom of God.
- being arrogant, exclusive and territorial.
- complacency: talking about things which need to be changed but not praying or doing anything about them.
- self-righteousness and making unrighteous judgments.
- being poor stewards over the land and squandering Your resources.
- leadership which has not followed God's Word.

We repent over—

- broken covenants in marriages which end in divorce.
- shedding of innocent blood through civil strife, violence, murder, addiction, family abuse and abortion.
- idolatry: anything we have put ahead of God, lust of the eye, lust of the flesh, pride of life.
- immorality: sexual impurity, pornography, adultery, fraud, theft, bearing false witness, exploiting the public trust.

Father, release Your grace of repentance upon the inhabitants of this city/place and cause it to return to You wholeheartedly.

We agree with the godly prayers of previous generations.

We call everything in darkness in this city/place to come into the light, and for the glory of God to fill the whole earth.

We pray that sins which have cursed the land be forgiven through repentance.

Kingdom of God, come to Earth!

PRAYER AT CITY GATES *(where main roads enter a city)*

We declare—

- that this city is under the sovereign control of Jesus Christ, His Blood is over it, and His sovereignty is over each soul.
- the blessing of unity. We call churches to come together and prepare for the harvest. We call the Body to wake up.
- strength to those who turn the battle at the gates.
- NO ACCESS TO TERROR IN THIS CITY!
- this city is the abode of the Holy Spirit.

We pray—

- Holy Spirit, perform a clean sweep of evil from this city.
- that awakening, revival and spiritual transformation take place in this city.
- that churches come together, righteousness reign, and wells of salvation and revival flow freely.
- for the government to have godly wisdom and spiritual insight to make this city safe.
- protection for all city employees including firefighters, police officers and public safety workers.
- that drownings, murders, suicides and accidental deaths will not take place in this city.
- safety on roads, highways, waterways and at airports.
- for the ministries in this city to have life, love souls and proclaim God's Word.
- that God assign angels as gatekeepers to encamp around this city, and that roots of corruption be exposed.

Give names to city gates, such as "Peace," "Truth," "Holiness," "Justice" and "Righteousness." Pray whenever you pass them.

Righteous Father, let Your name be glorified in this city. Rain down with extravagance Your grace, mercy and love.

DECLARATIONS FOR A CITY OR REGION

Father, break our hearts for the lost and blow the wind of Your Spirit across this region to stir us for righteous change.

The Blood of Jesus is against the spirit of death through violence, murder, abortion, addiction, sexual predators, pornography, and music which celebrates death.

We declare—
- Jesus Christ is Sovereign Lord over this city/region.
- an increase of the government and peace of Christ.
- the earth is the Lord's and the fullness thereof.
- this city's covenant with death is broken.
- awakening for the Body of Christ in this city/region.
- life to the waters, land and air in this city/region.

We pray—
- that abortions and shedding of innocent blood be stopped.
- that pastors have words of life, love souls, proclaim the truth of God, forsake ego and territorialism, and love one another.
- that city leaders have wisdom and insight to make this a safe and prosperous place.
- that all unbelievers in this city/region come into a saving knowledge of Jesus.
- that God raise up prayer warriors, intercessors, revivalists and fathers in the faith for this region.
- that people know the love and the Fatherhood of God.

We call—
- fathers to arise, come forth, take their rightful place and walk in the fulness of their destiny.
- people of this city/region into obedience to God's Word; and we pray they will prosper spiritually and financially.

NEIGHBORHOOD PRAYER WALK POINTS

We declare that—

• every household in this neighborhood is covered by the Blood of Jesus, which is the ultimate evidence of love, and overcomes all things harmful to us.

• Jesus is the head of every household.

• every family abide by the Ten Commandments—
"Have no gods before the True and Living God.
"Do not make, bow down to or serve graven images.
"Do not take the name of the Lord your God in vain.
"Remember to keep the Sabbath holy.
"Honor your fathers and mothers.
"Do not murder, commit adultery, steal, bear false witness or covet."

We pray—

• every family in this neighborhood bring up their children in the fear and admonition of the Lord.

• every father take his rightful place as spiritual leader, husband and parent.

• righteousness reign and rule in every home.

• the presence of God sanctify homes and families.

• every person have an overcoming testimony and the strength to endure to the end.

• safety, good health and the fruit of the Spirit for churches and pastors, school employees and students, and places where family members work.

• against idolatry, shedding of innocent blood, witchcraft, greed, rebellion, anger, hatred, unforgiveness, violence, addictions, blasphemy, lust, adultery, and all sexual sins.

PRAYERS FOR
Hospitals and Medical Facilities

We declare Jesus Christ is sovereign Lord and the Great Physician over this medical facility.

We pray for—

• wisdom, skill, humility, discernment, insight, knowledge and understanding for every staff member who diagnoses a condition or performs a procedure.

• staff and physicians to know The True and Living God, and have words of life for their patients.

• safety en route for every patient, family member and paramedic who arrives by ambulance, car or helicopter.

• miraculous healings.

• the compassion of Christ for all employees who work at this hospital.

• patients not to experience infections or other complications.

• staff to be alert to anything which could pose a danger to patients.

• chaplains to have words of life and comfort for patients and families.

• God to dispatch ministering angels to the suffering and grieving.

Lord, release the Spirit of Life to indwell this facility and dislodge all foul, hindering spirits and spirits of infirmity; and to create an atmosphere conducive to Your miraculous intervention.

PRAYERS FOR
Schools and Universities

We declare—

• that Jesus Christ is Sovereign Lord, the Way, the Truth and the Life; and the Holy Spirit is the Teacher.

• a mighty outpouring of God's Spirit.

• that awakening and revival will transform this campus into a place of holiness, reverence and righteousness.

• respect for the Word of God and the liberty to discuss it.

We pray for—

• students to hunger for the Truth and receive God's Spirit.

• the power and presence of Jesus Christ to be tangible.

• prodigals to return to the Lord.

• students and staff to know the love and Fatherhood of God.

• fear of God to fall on staff and students.

• renewed passion and zeal for Jesus Christ.

• godly sorrow over unbelief, rebellion and dissipation.

• students to be safe from harm and deception.

• addiction to drugs, alcohol, sex, pornography and other bondages to be replaced by devotion to God.

• the gift of evangelism to be imparted to students.

• this institution to produce missionaries and carriers of revival.

• campus ministries to be encouraged and effective.

• more and better attended prayer meetings on campus.

PRAYERS FOR RECONCILIATION OF THE RACES

We ask God's forgiveness for—

• broken covenants and inhumane policies toward Native and African Americans and other cultural groups.

• ethnic cleansing and forcing our culture on Native and African Americans in God's name.

• kidnapping Africans and Native Americans, and selling and buying them as slaves.

• brutal treatment of slaves, the sin of racism, and ongoing discrimination and mistrust of races toward one another.

We pray that—

• Native Americans respond to their God-given mandate as guardians of the land.

• all races know the True and Living God through His Son, Jesus.

• our government enact and enforce just policies toward all races and people.

• Native and African Americans and European descendants put away offense and forgive, love and trust one another.

• Africans, Native Americans and other nationalities receive their mantle from God as spiritual leaders in our culture.

• the Church set an example of moral justice and unity among the races.

We bless and give honor to—

• all ministries which have spent countless hours in intercession, preparing this nation for the glory of the Lord.

• churches, missionaries and ministries which have brought the Word of God and shepherded the flock.

Section 4

One Seamless Garment

Prayers

Name Your Gates & Take Back Your Cities

ONE SEAMLESS GARMENT PRAYERS

(Prayed at Maryland County Seats)

PROTECTION

Father, I pray to have our names and the names of our family members, our properties, what we are doing, every aspect of who we are – spirit, soul, and body – and all tracking avenues removed from hell and the realm of darkness. Jesus' Blood annuls all covenants with death and darkness and His Blood covers us. And hide us under the shadow of Your wings. Amen.

PRAYER TO LOVE THE BRIDE

Heavenly Father,

We bless Your Church, the Bride. Help us honor her and all her attendants. Help us not to split hairs over doctrine and tradition, and have true love for one another, and be patient and kind to other Christians who don't believe as we do.

Help us see the Body of Christ as a whole, not fragmented, so we will not be fragmented. Help us see Your Bride as glorious and beautiful. Help us attend to Your Bride, the Church.

Help us clear the slate of all offenses – past or ongoing – toward the Church, and write afresh on our slate, "LOVE."

We speak life to the Church and its shepherds. Help us honor and respect Your shepherds without idolatry. Help us love them and help them love each other.

One Seamless Garment Prayers

HARVEST PRAYER

Dear Heavenly Father, Lord of the Harvest:

- We desire Your heart and Your purposes.
- Restore families, awaken the Church, send revival.
- Open our eyes to the fields that are white unto harvest.
- Give us boldness and courage and wisdom to bring in the harvest.
- Help us be willing to be inconvenienced, to work hard and long to rescue the perishing.
- Help us encourage laborers to join with us.
- Renew our minds so we are not stuck in the past of how things used to be.
- Help us not be caught off guard.
- Give us the new tools You are using in this season.
- Help us gather the harvest from our schools, the foreigners among us and the backsliders, by demonstrating the love of Jesus, His mercy and grace.
- Forgive our laziness that makes us drag behind.
- Forgive us for loving our comfort, money and families more than the work of Your Kingdom.
- Forgive us for our prayerlessness, and help us desire to see Your Kingdom come no matter what the cost.
- Forgive us for not loving the whole Body of Christ, Your Church, in all its various family expressions; for criticizing each other and not reaching out to each other.

Name Your Gates & Take Back Your Cities

PRAYER FOR UNCOMMON FAITH

Dear Father in Heaven,

We call [CITY/COUNTY]:

• to uncommon faith and wholehearted devotion to You.

• into its godly destiny and authority – no longer can the forces of darkness rule here.

We declare [CITY/COUNTY] is a godly gateway of this region. We declare that Jesus Christ is Sovereign Lord and King and the only true authority of [CITY/COUNTY].

We agree with all the godly prayers that have been prayed here for lost family members and lost prosperity, and command the enemy to restore seven-fold what he hasa stolen from the residents of [CITY/COUNTY].

Prodigals and backsliders, return to your families! Love and forgiveness, flow! Respect and gratitude, flow! Finances, flow! Rivers of living water, flow! Justice, righteousness, strength and responsibility, flow!

We call you, [CITY/COUNTY], and all your residents to receive your sonship in Father God. You are not orphans, [CITY/COUNTY]. We call you to become sons of faith and sons of the covenant.

Every leader with a wrong motive that is harmful to the residents of [CITY/COUNTY], who does not have the people's best interest at heart, you must step down. We call righteous leaders to take their positions. Righteous leaders: Stop hiding and take your rightful places.

We declare [CITY/COUNTY] to be a model of righteousness, faith, justice and prosperity.

One Seamless Garment Prayers

DECLARATIONS FOR THE CITY/COUNTY

• We proclaim life in place of premature death, drownings, accidents, murder, abortion, addictions, abuse (physical, sexual and mental), pornography, and music which celebrates death.

• We pray that God send angels to drive out all rulers over addictions and occult powers.

• We pray that God send angels to incapacitate the worship of false gods (including vanity, money and possessions).

• We pray that God assign angels as gatekeepers to encamp around [CITY/COUNTY].

• We declare that the love of Christ abounds to [CITY/COUNTY] and overcomes sins associated with the spirit of death.

DECLARATIONS FOR THE PEOPLE

• We declare that death is stripped of its power to keep people in [CITY/COUNTY] bound by fear.

• We break the power of vain imaginations and everything which exalts itself against the knowledge of God.

• We break the assignments of spirits of bondage, heaviness, spiritual slumber, laziness, and a religious spirit. We send them back with their assignments unfulfilled.

• We pray that God's Spirit be fully released to operate unhindered in [CITY/COUNTY], convicting its people of righteousness, sin and judgment, and leading them into all truth.

• We declare reconciliation between men and God, and between individuals separated by unforgiveness, resentment, jealousy, bitterness, anger, violence, prejudice, pride, unholy judgments, etc.

Name Your Gates & Take Back Your Cities

DECLARATIONS FOR THE CHURCHES

- We declare resurrection to the Body of Christ in [CITY/COUNTY].
- The love of God indwell the churches, and come in the power of His Spirit to lead the people into all truth.
- The Church rise and shine forth the glory of the Lord, that leaders great and small be drawn to its brightness, her light break forth and her healing appear with righteousness, and the glory of the Lord be her rear guard.
- Intercessors, evangelists and harvesters: rise up in the Church with fresh vision and courage.
- Churches be revived, dryness and desolation break, and multiplied healings come.
- Release of the unhindered supply of heaven to the Church for all its needs.
- "The fire of the enemy shall be quenched, and revelation will enlighten us."
- The Church have a heart for all people, to meet them where they are.
- The Church experience victory breakthrough to advance the Kingdom of God.
- People in the churches know the Fatherhood of God, have encounters with His glory, and return to their First Love.
- People in the churches exhibit holiness, faithfulness, steadfastness, gratitude, single-mindedness, increased strength, courage and honesty.
- People in the churches undergo repentance, redemption, restoration and restitution.
- [CITY/COUNTY], prepare for your spiritual tsunami. The love of God is coming to you in a wave. It's God's time for you!

One Seamless Garment Prayers

PRAYER FOR BACKSLIDERS

Holy Spirit, bring backsliders to the cross. Reveal to them the love of Jesus and the Fatherhood of God. Deliver them from the orphan spirit and grant them the grace of repentance.

Deliver backsliders from disappointment, bitterness, shame and unforgiveness. Expose the enemy's lie of hopelessness and give them hope.

Father, pour out Your Spirit on them and fill them with light and life. Help them press into their destiny and forget the things of the past.

Save those who have never really given their hearts to You; in whom Your Word found nowhere to take root; for whom ridicule, abuse, fear, anger, selfishness, resentment, blaming or wealth have choked out the goodness You planted in them. Bring them back from captivity and gather them from all the places they have strayed. Help them humble themselves, seek You with their whole hearts, and make Jesus Savior and Lord.

Holy Spirit, guide them into all truth. Put a hunger in their hearts that can only be satisfied by You. Raise them up to advance the Kingdom of God. As You lead them into Your Kingdom, cause them to bring others in also, where there is righteousness, peace, joy and life forevermore.

For our part, forgive our dullness of spirit, lukewarmness, selfishness, lack of love, self-seeking and disinterest in prayer. Revive us and put fresh fire in us to love and serve You, and care for the souls of others.

Pour out Your Spirit on the backsliders and the unsaved, wake up Your Church, and raise up the harvesters.

Name Your Gates & Take Back Your Cities

PRAYER FOR FAMILIES AND FATHERS

Lord, please return the hearts of the fathers to their children. We pray they provide for, love and cherish them. Move fathers' hearts to repent for being absent physically, mentally or emotionally. Restore dignity and integrity to men.

Heal fathers of their own father wounds. Reveal to fathers when they are hurting their children in the same way they were hurt. Help fathers forgive their parents and those who wounded them or did not model righteousness, love, acceptance and fidelity.

Give men a heart of purity and compassion for children and single mothers. Give single mothers and fathers the desire to walk in obedience to Your Word. Wake up the Church to help provide the resources single parent families need.

Help children forgive their parents. Raise up substitutes for children whose fathers are estranged or no longer living. Pour out a great awareness of the Fatherhood of God.

Rescue whole families, even in the midst of desperate situations. Shine Your light, redeem and restore them. Pour out Your Spirit and reveal Your great love. Remove what is dead and prune what remains to bring forth abundant fruit.

Restore hope to mothers, fathers and children. Execute justice for the weak and the fatherless. Deliver them from wickedness.

We declare peace and restoration in family relationships. Cause fathers to be honest with themselves and acknowledge You so they will see gain and not loss.

Heal lives broken by divorce, abuse, anger and absent fathers. And heal children who don't know their fathers. Give wisdom to sons without a model of godly manhood. Help daughters with father-hunger, who are looking for men to love them, to possess modesty and chastity.

Heal and deliver parents and children who are addicted to

One Seamless Garment Prayers

drugs or alcohol. Holy Spirit, be such a presence in their lives that they cannot deny You.

Father of all and full of mercy, help us see our sins and repent. Be gracious and forgive us. Rescue families from the clutches of hell and show the way back to You. Hear the pleas of Your remnant and cause the world to cry out to You.

Father, give the churches a fresh burden for families through prayer and action. Restore families. Awaken Your Church. Send revival.

DECLARATIONS FOR THE LAND

• We break the power of all curses on the land and the people, and all unholy covenants.

• We declare the superior covenant, which Jesus purchased with His Blood, that reconciles men to God.

We declare—

Churches come together.
Righteousness prevail.
Wells of revival flow.
Backsliders and prodigals return.
Families be restored.
Fathers protect their families.
Church, awaken!

Name Your Gates & Take Back Your Cities

PRAYER FOR COMMUNITIES

Protect members of the law enforcement and military communities. Give them discernment, wisdom and mercy. Help them walk in peace and justice. Give them increased courage and determination to do the job You have created them for. Give them favor, support and honor in the communities they serve.

Give law enforcement divine strategies to make their cities safe and peaceful places in which to dwell. Let them be seen as officers of peace and not the enemy. Station mighty warrior angels with each one. Surround them with a shield of love, power and discipline that cannot be penetrated by evil forces. Protect them in their homes from sabotage by the enemy that would bring disunity into their families. Protect their children from drug and alcohol abuse.

Heal and deliver addicted people in our communities, and turn their addiction to Jesus, righteousness, holiness and revival. Cause love and generosity to replace heroin and other drugs. Give the law enforcement and medical communities and all emergency responders wisdom to deal with the drug issue.

Infiltrate gangs with Your love, that they will know the Fatherhood of God, have hope for a good future, and totally turn their lives around. Heal their hurts and cause them to understand they are valuable to You and Your Kingdom. Put them in righteous settings, and raise up spiritual fathers and mothers to mentor and love them.

Awaken the churches to needs in their communities, and raise them up to fervently pray.

One Seamless Garment Prayers

CHILDREN'S PRAYER

Father God, we plead the Blood of Jesus and a hedge of protection around our children and all the children of this generation. Do a mighty work to bring forth revival through them.

Cause them to have wisdom to recognize and obey Your call on their lives. Cause them to be disenchanted with worldly knowledge and seek the true Source of Power.

Cause children to learn from You, recognize Your voice, and discern Your will. Help them find the humility to understand the Truth. Cause their feet to walk in righteousness.

We pray children have unstopped ears to hear You, and be sensitive and receptive to the Holy Spirit. Give them a burning desire to know and love You.

Cause them to become the leaders and fishers of men You created them to be. And cause them to manifest temperance, patience, integrity and peace.

We pray the issues of their hearts be goodness, peace and mercy, and that they hunger for holiness, desire to serve You, loathe evil, and desire good.

REQUESTING THE KINGDOM

We invite the Kingdom of God.
We request the Kingdom of God.
We claim the Kingdom of God.
We declare the Kingdom of God.
We release the Kingdom of God.

Name Your Gates & Take Back Your Cities

PRAYER FOR REVELATION

We pray that a revelation of the goodness and love of the Father be poured out on those who have believed the devil's lies.

For children and adults who don't have a positive, godly image of themselves, we pray they receive their true identity as sons and daughters of their Loving Father through the Blood that Jesus shed on the cross.

We pray they know that God their Father wants them to come into His Kingdom, where there is plenty of love and forgiveness for all.

COMMISSION FOR MEN AND BOYS TO BE SPIRITUAL FATHERS

We call for sons to become spiritual fathers. It is Father God's good pleasure to give you His Kingdom: righteousness, peace and joy in the Holy Spirit.

We declare:

- God loves you.
- He has chosen you out of the world.
- You belong to Him.
- You have worth in the Kingdom of God.
- The Truth sets you free.

One Seamless Garment Prayers

DECLARATIONS FOR FAMILIES

Arise, fathers! Come forth! Take your rightful place of leadership in your homes and in the Body of Christ! Be the priest, husband and parent God intends you to be! Walk in God's calling and fulfill your destiny!

By the Blood of Jesus, we break the power of bloodline iniquities of the fathers over families. We come against homosexuality, incest and all forms of perversion in all the power of the Name and Blood of Jesus Christ, and break its power over families.

We call families and fathers to meditate on that which is true, noble, just, pure, lovely, of good report, virtuous and praiseworthy.

MORE PRAYERS ARE IN SECTION 3 OF THIS BOOK

We would love to hear your testimonies of praying at your gates. Please send reports and photos to—

NameYourGates@comcast.net.

Shiloh Books

Name Your Gates & Take Back Your Cities – 90 pages
An activation manual to focus your prayer life, gain territory for God's Kingdom, and declare His sovereignty in your gates.

$12 each *(includes shipping)*

Things Hoped For – 25 years of prophetic wisdom and encounters with God – two books in one – 304 pages.
Readers are saying—

"It is the most profoundly faith-building book I have ever read."
"It was delightfully refreshing, enlightening, and very sobering."
"…a good book for people who are struggling with their Christian walk."
"Excellent resource for intercessory prayer…"

$15 each *(includes shipping)*

Where Do You Hurt? Where Do You Hide? – 58 pages
Fear and shame erect a NO TRESPASSING sign to God as we try to hide parts of us we don't want to surrender to Him. This is a guide to come out of hiding and into God's destiny for your life.

$10 each *(includes shipping)*

The Rehearsal or Living Life Live – 48 pages
Overcome fear of the unknown. This booklet recounts the tests and breakthroughs when God said, "Stop rehearsing the future."

$10 each *(includes shipping)*

Timeless Wisdom – three 48-page booklets of messages from the Lord on *Kingdom Living*, *Prosperous Living* and *Revival Living*.

$10 for the set *(includes shipping)*

Send checks to:
Shiloh Ministries, 209 West St., Berlin, MD 21811
E-mail: NameYourGates@comcast.net